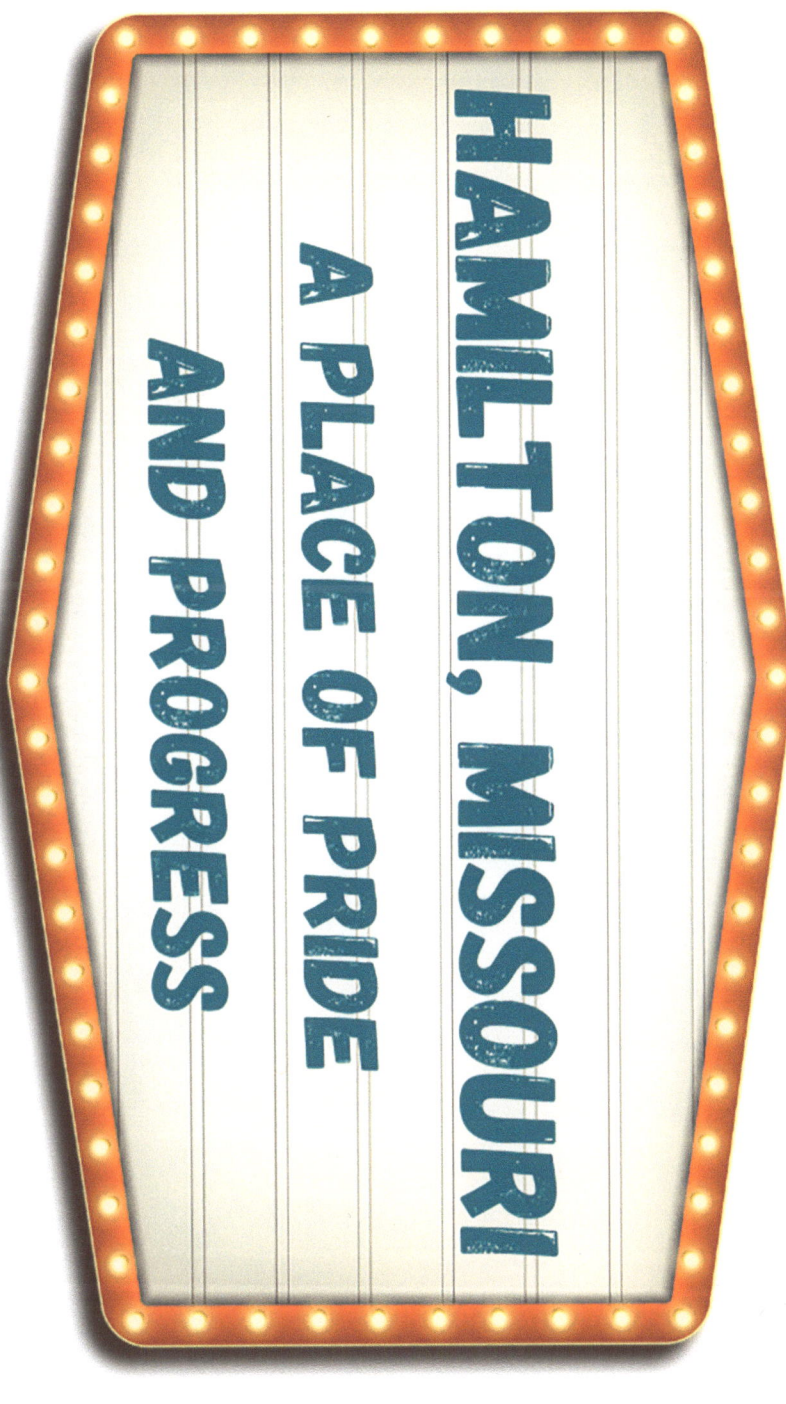

HAMILTON, MISSOURI

A PLACE OF PRIDE

AND PROGRESS

By Dennis Cox

Anne Spry, Editor

Published by Personal Chapters LLC

2024

Hamilton, Missouri: A Place of Pride and Progress

By Dennis Cox

Edited by Anne Spry

Foreword by Jenny Doan

Copyright 2024 by Personal Chapters LLC

All Rights Reserved

Printed in the U. S. A.

Hardcover ISBN: 979-8-9889980-8-2

Paperback ISBN: 979-8-9911560-5-9

Library of Congress Control Number: 2024913554

Cover Image taken from sections of a community mural in Hamilton, MO by late artist Kelly Poling

Cover Design by Anne Spry

Published by Personal Chapters LLC

Independence, MO and Wakarusa, KS

A NOTE FROM THE AUTHOR...

Thirty years ago, I expressed my feelings that there were probably enough Hamilton photos and memories "out there" for one or two more volumes of a history book. I never guessed, at the time, that I would get the opportunity to do this all over again.

There are so many people to thank for their contributions, directly and indirectly, to this 2024 updated edition of Hamilton historical memories.

In editing and revising this edition, there were so many more avenues open for research than when the first book was published over 30 years ago at the Hamilton Advocate.

So open up and begin turning the pages. You'll find more photos, more updated and descriptive text and more pages of historical memories, some familiar and some completely unexpected.

Foremost, when handing out thank yous, I must first thank my wife, Joyce, for allowing me the space, the support and minimal distractions while working on this project a second time.

Thanks to the ladies at Caldwell County Abstract & Title, Caldwell County Assessor and Recorder's offices for their help in tracking down information on eighty homes and homeowners you will find inside.

Finally, thanks to Anne Spry for her publishing expertise and her willingness to revisit this project after so long. It was fun slipping back into that old, familiar working relationship.

Finally, here's to the future growth and prosperity for the City of Hamilton, even as we remember and hang on to the memories of the past!

–Dennis Cox

Dennis Cox

... AND THE PUBLISHER

Years before we sold the newspaper in Hamilton and retired to Kansas City, Jenny Doan had often asked me if there were any copies of *Hamilton Historical Highlights* hidden somewhere, because she sure wanted to buy them. The answer was always a "No, sorry."

In the intervening years, I moved even further away from Hamilton than Kansas City...all the way to Wakarusa, KS., where my father's family had homesteaded. By then I had found my way into the book publishing business as a retirement career.

One day Fran Esry sent a private Facebook message on Jenny's behest and asked about that history book again. A few weeks later, Dennis Cox called. It was time to revive this project that Hamilton business owners and history buffs had been pushing for. The first book, done way back in the 1990s, was followed years later by a Sesquicentennial reprint.

For the first book, Dennis spent countless hours in the darkroom making prints from glass negatives. For this book everything is digital and done on a computer. While producing any book is still labor intensive, it was a bit easier the third time around. It was a joy to work again with Dennis and revisit virtually the places and faces I came to know and love while living in Hamilton and publishing the newspaper for 27 years. What I love the most is that the community is still thriving after surviving some difficult economic downturns. And as I put this book together, I was gratified to once again make connections with a place and with people that occupied so many chapters of my own history

Anne Spry

–Anne Spry

FOREWORD: THE ENDURING SPIRIT OF HAMILTON

As I reflect on my nearly three decades in Hamilton, I am filled with a profound sense of gratitude for this charming town that has become our home. Since our family's arrival in 1995, Hamilton has not only been a place of residence but a sanctuary--a nurturing environment where we've watched our children grow and become integral parts of the community fabric.

I've always felt a deep reverence for the history of Hamilton. It's a history woven into the very walls of the old homes we've lovingly restored, each creak and crack telling tales of generations past. My fascination with the stories of those who shaped our town, their aspirations, struggles, and triumphs, has only deepened over the years.

Thus, it is with immense excitement that I welcome the reprinting of this book, a testament to the enduring spirit of Hamilton. Through its pages, we are granted a glimpse into the bygone eras, where the echoes of bustling businesses and the laughter of families still resonate. The photographs captured within these chapters not only depict structures but serve as windows of the past, inviting us to immerse ourselves in the rich tapestry of our town's history.

I am thrilled to know that there are individuals among us who share this passion

for preservation, who understand the value of honoring our heritage and strive to safeguard it for future generations. Their dedication to maintaining the integrity of our historic homes and businesses is a source of inspiration and a testament to the enduring legacy of community pride.

As we embark on this journey through time, may we cherish the stories within these pages, and may they serve as a reminder of the resilience, ingenuity, and unwavering spirit of the people who call Hamilton home. Together, let us continue to preserve, celebrate, and enrich the legacy of our beloved town for years to come.

Jenny Doan

Jenny Doan, Hamilton resident and the face of Missouri Star Quilt Company

Hamilton, Missouri–A Place of Pride Then and Now

Maybe you're just a visitor. Or perhaps you live in Hamilton or Caldwell County, or once did. No matter your connection to this place, you'll find much to be proud of in Hamilton's history, and even more to enjoy if you're just here for a short time.

In the pages that follow you will find a pictorial history of Hamilton, interspersed with photos of modern-day points of pride. This is a bustling place now, just as it was at many times in its history. It's full of hard-working, enterprising folks now, just as it eventually became when Albert Gallatin Davis founded it back in the fall of 1854. In its heyday at the turn of the century, Hamilton's main street was a source of pride with its many Victorian buildings offering a variety of goods and services. Following many economic downturns that occurred (once when the railroad abandoned the line through town, and again when

the International Shoe Company factory closed its doors) Hamilton has once again enjoyed a resurgence as the new "Quilt Town USA."

The railroad that once came through town is the reason Hamilton exists. You'll now find a mural on the side of the Missouri Star Quilt Company headquarters building depicting the importance of the Hannibal & St. Joseph Railroad. When the company was surveying land through Caldwell County in 1851 to build it, the town of Hamilton was nothing but unbroken prairie. It surrounded an old pioneer trail that ran from Gallatin in the north to Lexington in the south. Hunters and trappers used the area that would become Hamilton as a temporary stopping place in their wanderings.

One old story recalls a trapper named Nixon who lived in a shack near the present site of Missouri Star Quilt headquarters prior to 1854. He reportedly had deer feeding in his yard every day and he shot many bears nearby. The story goes that when he learned the railroad would pass through his front yard, he moved on.

The Hamilton Town Company was formed in the fall of 1854 for the purpose of locating a town along the railroad. This group was composed of Edward Samuel, Greenup Bird, John Berry, Michael Arthur, Simpson McGaughy and Stephen Richey, all of Liberty; John Ardinger and Ephraim Ewing, Richmond; Charles J. Hughes, Kingston; Thomas T. Frame, Gallatin; John Burrows, Mirable; Jeff Thomson, St. Joseph; and a Mirable farmer, surveyor and former soldier named Albert Gallatin Davis.

The town company originally planned to purchase land from the railroad and located the town where Nettleton now stands but Davis, seeking a leading role in development of the new community, learned of a tract of land that had not been entered by the railroad. The town company had already entered the land on both sides of the non-entered tract and Davis knew the land would come cheaper from the government than from private owners.

Davis set out about 9 p.m. on a fall evening and, by surveying successfully, located the tract in question. He immediately sent his

A mural on the side of the headquarters of Missouri Star Quilt Company depicts the history of Hamilton, MO as a railroad town. Even though the railroad is gone, the town is still a busy place full of visitors. Today they come in private cars and trucks instead of by rail.

construction—laying ties on lumps of frozen ground and cobbling the rails together in hurried fashion in order to win the wager of ten gallons of whiskey.

Originally, the railroad intended to lay track one block north of the site they finally chose and as a result, many of the first businesses and buildings in town were built on or closer to Bird St. in anticipation. The first train depot was built in the fall of 1859 and A. G. Davis was the first railroad and express agent. Prior to the building of the depot, freight was piled on the ground near the track and a guard was hired to watch it until owners took it away.

Hamilton's early growth was slow. Only about 25 families made their home in the town of the late 1850s and early 1860s but farmhouses stood nearby on all sides. The town held its own in population during the war years and remained loyal to the Union, with a few Rebel sympathizers in the area. The first federal troops regularly stationed here were a company of the 50th Illinois and some of James' battalion of Home Guards. These came in 1861 and, thereafter, the town was seldom without Yankee troops.

After the war, many soldiers on each side of the fighting—North and South—returned to their homes but were either discontented with or could not readjust to their old lives. Seeking a place to put down new roots for their families, many found such an opportunity in Hamilton.

From 1859 to 1877, four additions were added to the original town plat—Hillsborough (1859), the Railroad Addition (1867), Samuel's (1868), and Miller's (1877). As the town prospered, the necessity for a more efficient form of city government became apparent. On Aug. 3, 1868, a petition was presented to the county court asking it to declare Hamilton a corporation under laws of the state. George Lamson, Anthony Rohrbough, F.P. Low, John N. Morton and William Partin were named the first trustees.

In the fall of 1865, the first public schoolhouse was erected on the site of the Methodist Church parsonage. Prior to that, school was held on the second floor of John Morton's tin shop located on the north lot of today's Hamilton Lumber Company. Mrs. Elizabeth Morton Lenderson, a sister to Morton and a Civil War widow, was the first teacher at the Morton school. The new schoolhouse added to the prosperity of the town by

6

Albert Galltin Davis (1818—1908) is considered Hamilton's founding father.

nephew, Tilton Davis, to the land office in Plattsburg upon learning his suspicions were confirmed. The land was entered in the name of Samuel, president of the Hamilton Town Company. Prairie City was the name for the town favored by most of the company, but Davis received the honor of christening the town "Hamilton," partly in honor of the statesman Alexander Hamilton, and partly for Joseph Hamilton, a brilliant lawyer and noted soldier whom Davis admired.

Forty acres was laid off into lots and blocks in the spring of 1855, and the first sale of lots was held in October. The sale was widely advertised and attended by a large crowd who partook of the free dinner and free whiskey provided by the town company. Judge Parrott of Plattsburg was the auctioneer and bidding was lively. John Berry purchased the first lot.

The first house in Hamilton was built by Davis and stood on the north half of the Hy-Klas parking lot location. The pine lumber used in the home was purchased in St. Louis, shipped up the Missouri River on a steamboat to Camden in Ray County, then hauled in wagons drawn by oxen to Hamilton. The Davis home became known as the "Lone House" because of its isolation on the prairie and for many years was used as an overnight hotel by passengers on the stage line. It took a day to make the trip one way from Gallatin to Lexington, and one to return.

In the 1860s, the hotel changed hands and became known as the Claypool Hotel. Miss Mary Gartland of Carrollton taught school in the Davis home to children of the Davis family and some others.

The railroad was completed through Hamilton on Feb. 14, 1859, and the first engine came in from the West on the very next day. The railroad company had made a bet with the contractors that the track would not be ready for the engine by Saint Valentine's Day so the contractors rushed drawing more settlers to the community. Following on by the financial panic of 1873, progress of the town was rapid. Brick store buildings began replacing old one- and two-story frames. Major fires to the business district in 1883, 1884 and 1886 also accelerated the change to modern structures.

A.C. Cochran of Ohio established the first bank in Caldwell County in a brick building located on today's site of the Hy-Klas Food and Family Center parking lot. In 1873, Anthony Rohrbough built the second brick business building in town, later known as the Anderson building, on the southeast corner of Davis and Bird streets.

Hamilton, during the first two decades following the Civil War, was a bustling business center for the county with the establishment of liveries, lumberyards, grain elevators and the Hamilton Roller Mill. Livestock producers took advantage of the railroad in getting their produce to markets in Saint Joseph, Kansas City and Chicago. Early dry goods and mercantile houses dealt in groceries, clothing, hardware, farm tools and machinery and offered other services to early pioneers. The town now had bankers, lawyers, doctors, a dentist, photographer and two newspapers, the News-Graphic and Hamiltonian. The Hamilton House, built in 1866, offered a rest stop for those traversing the old pioneer road from Gallatin to Lexington. Later boarding houses were the Western House and Broadway Hotel.

Hamilton experienced perhaps its biggest growth period from 1880– when it became a city of the fourth class–to 1900. A third newspaper, the Farmer's Advocate, sprang to life in 1890 to champion the workers cause. The Hamilton District Fair Association was formed in November of 1882 and the first fair, held in 1883, drew thousands of spectators. The Hamilton Chautauqua (1907-18), North Missouri Fair (1919-31), American Legion Race Meet (1932-50) and North Missouri Steam and Gas Engine Show (1963-90) have successfully carried on a 100-year-old tradition of outdoor entertainment.

The Hamilton Coal and Caldwell Coal companies employed hundreds of workers around the turn of the century and the town could also boast of such industries as the Hamilton Electric Company, Hamilton Telephone Company, Hamilton Creamery Company, Hamilton Manufacturing Company, Hamilton Sawmill, a

cheese factory, canning factory, cigar factory and cider mill.

As the early years of the 20th Century passed, stores began specializing in only one line of merchandise. By then the advent of the internal combustion engine signaled the end of horse-drawn and steam-powered forms of work and travel.

Hamilton residents voted $5,000 in bonds for construction of a city hall in 1911, and with the help of J. C. Penney, built a public library in 1920. Waterworks and sewer bonds were issued in 1924 and in 1926, aldermen passed a resolution to pave five blocks of Davis Street from the Congregational Church north to the site of the old Paxton livery barn. Many of the town's finest homes were built in the period between 1890 and 1920. Many of those homes are still standing today and are sources of pride for their owners and Hamiltonians in general.

The Hamilton Development Corporation and J. C. Penney, perhaps Hamilton's most famous son, were instrumental in persuading the International Shoe Company to build a manufacturing plant in Hamilton in 1947. Penney and his family were also large contributors to the construction of Penney High School in 1949.

Hamilton District Fair. The Hamilton District Fair was formed in November of 1882, and the first fair was held in 1883 on 70 acres of land purchased from A. G. Davis. Easily, recognizable is today's site of the PHS football field and stadium.

Timeline of Hamilton and National Events

Hamilton Event	Year	U.S. Event
A.G. Davis surveys future site of Hamilton	1854	First U.S. Naval Academy graduating class
First store in Hamilton north of depot	1857	14th Amendment to the Constitution adopted
Hannibal & St. Joseph Railroad completed	1859	Discovery of the Comstock Lode in Utah
Federal troops stationed in Hamilton	1861	Confederate attack on Fort Sumpter
First public school established	1865	Assassination of President Lincoln
North Side school built	1871	First Major League baseball game played
Family of banker William T. Kemper moves	1873	Levi Strauss begins manufacturing jeans
First Hamilton District Fair established	1882	Jesse James shot in St. Joseph, Mo.
Hamilton incorporated as 4th class city	1886	Dedication of the Statue of Liberty
Hamilton & Kingston Railroad established	1890	Yosemite designated a National Park
Hamilton Telephone Company established	1890	Wounded Knee massacre in South Dakota
Highland Cemetery incorporated	1912	U. S. Senate begins Titanic investigation
Hamilton Light & Power Co. incorporated	1914	Babe Ruth debuts with the Boston Red Sox
First Hamilton Public Library	1920	Women gain the right to vote
J. C. Penney Store opens in Hamilton	1924	First Macy's Thanksgiving Parade in NYC
First issue of water and sewer bonds	1924	J. Edgar Hoover appointed head of the FBI
HHS chooses "Hornets" as official mascot	1925	First Grand Ole Opry radio broadcast
First "talkies" movie at McBrayer Theatre	1930	Col. Sanders opens first KFC in Corbin, Ky.
International Shoe Co. begins operations	1947	Jackie Robinson becomes first black MLB player

8

Year	Hamilton Event	National/World Event
1948	American Legion Hall dedicated	Beginning of the Berlin blockade
1955	Week long Centennial celebration	Rosa Parks refused to give up bus seat to a white woman
1956	Lakeview Golf Course opens	Elvis Presley enters the charts with "Heartbreak Hotel"
1962	Cardinal Lanes opens	Cuban Missile Crisis
1964	First North Missouri Steam & Gas show	Martin Luther King gives "I Have A Dream" speech
1964	Municipal swimming pool opens	Pres. Johnson signs the Civil Rights Act
1967	Hillcrest Nursing Home opens	Beatles release "Sgt. Pepper's Lonely Hearts Club Band"
1971	Death of J. C. Penney	"All In The Family" debuts on CBS
1972	New city hall erected	Five Watergate burglars arrested
1976	Dedication of new J. C. Penney Museum	First outbreak of Legionnaire's disease in Philadelphia
1977	First PHS state basketball championship	Star Wars released by 20th Century Fox
1981	Local J. C. Penney Store closes	Last Walter Kronkite appearance on CBS Evening News
1988	Penney Boyhood Home moved to town	Iran-Contra Affair
1993	New Middle School building completed	Great Flood of Missouri and Mississippi rivers
1993	Hamilton Hotel demolished	Strategic Arms Reduction Treaty with Russia
2005	Week long Sesquicentennial celebration	Hurricane Katrina devastates New Orleans
2008	Missouri Star Quilt Co. established	Barak Obama sworn in as first African-American president
2009	First PHS state football title	20th year celebration of the fall of the Berlin Wall
2009	Hamilton Elementary School completed	US Flight 1549 ditches in the Hudson River
2014	Levi Garrison & Sons opens in telephone bldg.	First ebola case diagnosed in the U.S.
2023	New High School building completed	Criminal proceedings begin in Jan. 6 US Capitol attack

MISSOURI STAR QUILT COMPANY

The Missouri Star Quilt Company headquarters is located on Davis Street and is where the company expanded when it became more than a longarm quilting operation that began as a "hobby" for Jenny Doan.

This Mercantile Store offers shoppers a unique, old-fashioned setting for mostly modern items. It is just one of many Hamilton storefronts that has been refurbished and modernized by MSQC.

Hamilton's Davis Street features many stores related to sewing and quilting. During peak tourist season, the streets are full of shoppers.

The Missouri Star Quilt Company (MSQC) has made Hamilton the "Quilt Capital of the World." From one building in 2008 to a dozen shops, two large warehouses catering to online customers, MSQC has revitalized Hamilton's main street and made it and the town a destination for visitors from all 50 states and a large number of countries around the world.

In 2008, Ron and Jenny Doan bought the building on the corner of Berry and Ardinger Streets to house a longarm quilting machine. From there the company grew into a family business and MSQC quickly became the biggest quilting channel on YouTube.

MSQC today has one of the largest and best selections of quilting fabric online and in shops. The Sewing Center on Hamilton's main street offers space for quilting retreats. The Missouri Star Quilt Company today is the biggest employer in Caldwell County.

This quilt shop is housed in the former JCPenney store.

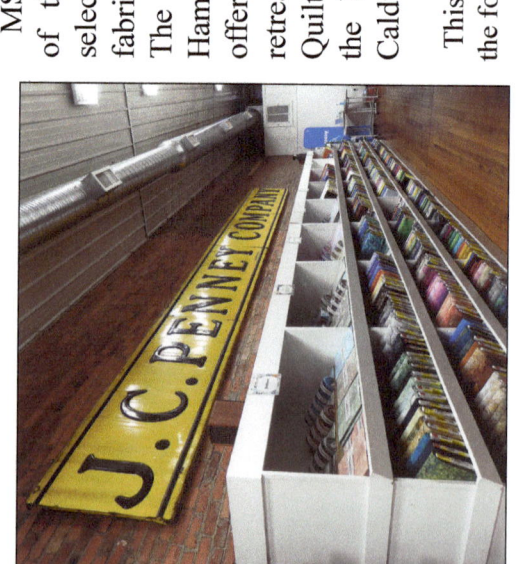

Missouri Quilt Museum

The Missouri Quilt Museum opened in the former Hamilton Elementary School (previously the high school). The mission of the non-profit museum is to depict the history of quilting and sewing in North America by offering visual and interactive opportunities that educate and engage visitors in experiences that encourage an active interest in quilting and sewing. It is supported by donations.

Left: The Missouri Bicentennial Quilt is a project of the State Historical Society of Missouri and Missouri Star Quilt Company in partnership with Missouri State Quilters Guild.

Hundreds of toy sewing machines are displayed in one of the first floor rooms.

A third floor room features the "Einstein" quilt with vintage quilts.

Right: The largest spool of thread welcomes visitors to the remodeled Hamilton Elementary building.

FROM A FRONTIER TOWN TO A BUSY COMMERCIAL CENTER

Bustling frontier town. This photo, taken in 1868, is the oldest known picture of early Hamilton. It looks north from a vantage point near the Broadway Hotel (old Hawks Building).

Granitoid sidewalk. W. W. Anderson was one of the first Hamilton merchants to lay a concrete sidewalk in front of his store in the spring of 1900.

Skyline view. At the age of 17, Dr. Foster E. Ackley began studying medicine with Drs. Donaldson and Lindley. He opened the Squibb Pharmacy in 1891 and put many preparations on the market, including "Skunk Oil Liniment." This view looks south from the roof of the Burlington Hotel, over the Naugle Elevator. A man on a ladder paints the north side of the Savoy Hotel. The windmill on top of the McBrayer Livery Stable can be seen against the middle skyline.

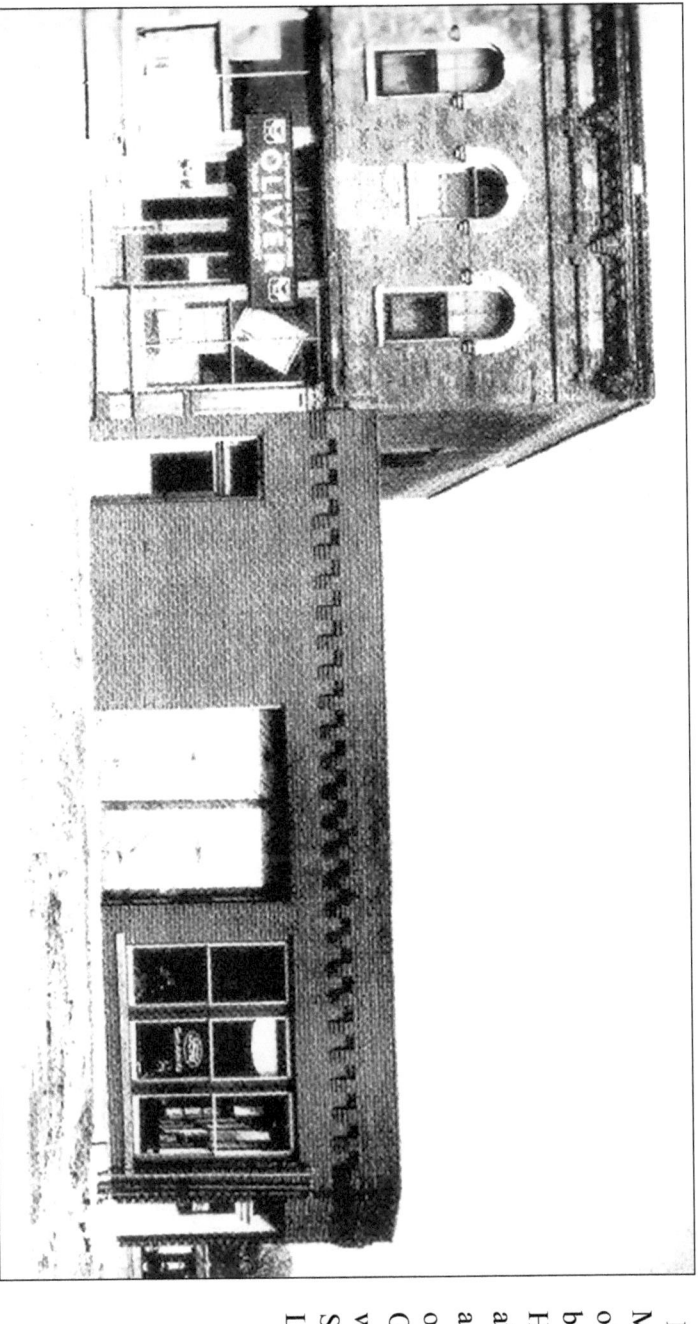

Hawks Motor Company. Fred Hawks founded Hawks Motor Company in 1910, first selling Everett Touring Cars. He opened his first garage in 1912 in a two-story frame building on Davis Street that later housed Couch Motors, Irwin Motors and is now the site of Missouri Star Quilt Company's main shop. Hawks rented the L. L. Grigsby building in 1914 and moved to the corner of Ardinger and Berry streets, adding the Ford line that year. This is the original site of the 1870 Broadway Hotel. Lee Souders bought the building when Hawks moved to the new dealership site in 1920. Davis Motors rented the building for a Ford dealership from 1930 to 1942.

Hamlet Building. Lynn Hamlet leased Ester Martin's building on North Davis for his line of Allis-Chalmers farm equipment in 1944 but bought the Souders building next to the old Hawks site in 1945. He tore down a large porch at the rear and added a new addition, as well as a new stairway to the second floor. This was the original site of David Buster's home in 1859. O. O. Brown built the brick building in 1878. Later it was a grocery store and upstairs residence of Dr. S. V. Stoller. In 1905, Stoller sold the building to L. L. Grigsby.

Dr. Tinsley Brown. Seated fourth from the left on the second row, Dr. Tinsley Brown was honored in 1926 for his 50 years of medical practice in Hamilton. This photo was taken in front of his home, once the Joseph Anderson home and now home of the Westover family. Others in this photo are: Dr. Lyle Daley, extreme left on the back row; Dr. and Mrs. Lee J. Eads, fourth and fifth from the left on the back row; Elmer Clark, fifth man from left on the back row (mustached); J. W. McLean, eighth man from left on the back row. Pictured on the front row are: Merle Brown, second from left; James Brown, fifth from left; Menzie Brown next to James, and Gail Brown, third from right. Mrs. Tinsley Brown is seated to the doctor's right.

14

Blacksmith Shop. An early Hamilton blacksmith shop, possibly located on East Berry Street.

North Missouri Lumber: This site has always been a lumber yard, beginning with Samuel Baldwin's (backed by Hamilton founder A.G. Davis) in 1858. George Reddie bought the lumberyard in 1866 and operated it until 1898 when it was purchased by the Hannibal Saw Mill Co. Soon after, its name was changed to the North Missouri Lumber Company. John Cowley was manager at the time of the 1918 fire that destroyed the buildings and contents.

Novelty Works. The Hamilton Novelty Works occupied a two-story frame building facing Berry Street behind the brick building at the northeast corner of the Davis and Berry intersection. William Moffit was proprietor of the business, established in 1880.

HAMILTON CHAUTAUQUA—1907 TO 1918

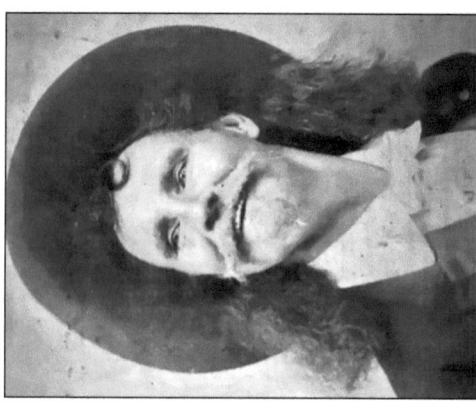

Capt. Jack Crawford, 1910

William Jennings Bryan, 1909

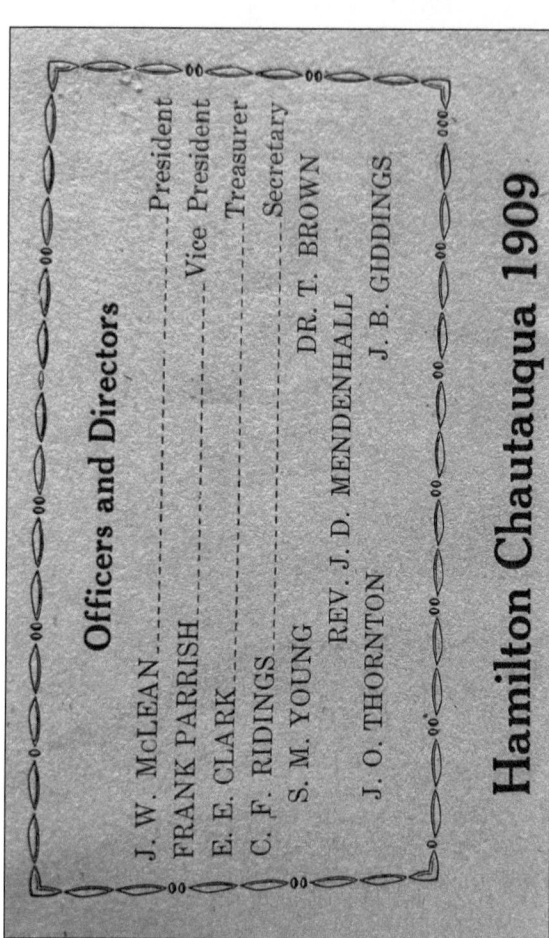

Officers and Directors

J. W. McLEAN ———————— President
FRANK PARRISH ————— Vice President
E. E. CLARK ——————————— Treasurer
C. F. RIDINGS ——————————— Secretary
S. M. YOUNG   DR. T. BROWN
              REV. J. D. MENDENHALL
      J. O. THORNTON   J. B. GIDDINGS

Hamilton Chautauqua 1909

"A 9 Days Outing, Pleasure, Recreation, Education."

The first annual Hamilton Chautauqua Assembly advertised its purpose on the front cover of its program. The idea of holding the asssembly was advanced by businessmen and local citizens who set up a guaranty fund of $3,500 to engage speakers and set up an organization.

The event, held either at the city park or the fairgrounds, became a favorite time for families to vacation and get educated, informed and entertained at the same time. A sea of white tents marked the grounds as families set up camp for a few days, overnight or the entire nine days of the lecture and music events.

Oratory was prized in the early 1900s when the Chautauqua was big in Hamilton. William Jennings Bryan was probably the most famous orator to grace the Hamilton Chauqauqua platform. Other programs included children's story hours, bands and orchestras, and even an occasional comedy team.

The Hamilton Chautauqua continued until 1918, when the program even included six nights of "moving pictures." The theme of the program that year was patriotism. America was in World War I, and the organizers said they were cooperating with the government in every way to teach and preach patriotism. The program noted, "The Chautauqua, in the words of President Wilson, has become an integral part of the national defense."

That was the last year for the Hamilton Chautauqua. The North Missouri Fair in 1919 took its place, and county and local residents traded chautauqua education and oratory for contests, livestock events and high-flying trapese artists.

Chautauqua Grove–This photo taken in 1908 shows a wealth of shade trees near the south end of the old wooden grandstand.

1908 Hamilton Chautauqua–The Hamilton race track was overgrown with tall grass and wasn't used during Hamilton's second annual Chautauqua Assembly in 1908.

Attending the Fair–A family poses in front of the old judge's stand on the Hamilton fairgrounds, probably during one of the Hamilton Chautauqua celebrations.

Ice Cream Parlor–Young people attending the 1908 Hamilton Chautauqua sample some of the tastier treats provided by one of the booths.

Watermelon break. A group of ladies enjoy a watermelon break behind the grandstand during the 1908 Chautauqua.

Knights of Pythias. Many fraternal organizations, including the Knights of Pythias, set up tents for the 1908 Chautauqua.

Hamilton Band. Members of the Hamilton Concert Band of 1902 and 1903 include Lee Dudley, Luke Williams, Frank Gibson, Sherm Green, Jim Allee, Carl Pease, Will Hare, Will Howard, Clarence Bainter, Earl Howard and Clarence Greene.

18

Early Construction Activity

Rauber and Johnson. The masonry contracting firm of John Rauber and Charles Johnson did more to lay the "foundation" of Hamilton than all others combined. They built most of the granitoid sidewalks in town, including this one in front of the old Baptist Church, and laid many of the foundations for Hamilton's oldest homes and business houses.

George Reddie home. The George Reddie home was built during the 1860s and stood on the lot at the northeast corner of Davis and Samuel Streets. Guy Thomson bought the property in 1916 and tore down the old home to build a modern one. Reddie was the proprietor of the old Chicago Lumber Yard established in 1866.

This 1920s photo of the Martin Grocery Store shows Latimer Martin on the far right and Chet Mart in the middle background wearing a dark suit.

Hamilton Churches
Then and Now

United Methodist Church. The Hamilton United Methodist Church was built in 1868 at a cost of $3,700 and used until 1899 when the present brick building was dedicated. The first church bell weighed 600 pounds and cost $130. The old parsonage, a two-story, ten-room house built in 1881, was moved to South Hughes Street in 1953 by C. J. Gurley in order for the present parsonage to be built. The foundation of the old house was built of native stone 16 inches wide, 14 inches thick and from three to seven feet long. The original parsonage stood on a lot north of the present church.

Railroad. Foundations for the present church building (top right inset) were laid during 1895 and building construction occurred between 1899 and 1900 at a cost of $7,054. The first church service was held on December 2, 1900, and the building was dedicated on May 12, 1901. The Fellowship Hall addition was dedicated in October of 1967. The classroom wing was completed during June of 1991.

Church Merger. The First Presbyterian Church (bottom right) was organized on August 16, 1867, with the First Congregational Church (top left) organized in February of 1899. Both churches recorded earlier services being held in members' homes or other area churches. According to old records, the First Congregational Church and Hamilton Disciples of Christ merged on November 27, 1891. The First Presbyterian Church and Congregational Church merged in February of 1928 when members of the Presbyterian Church locked the doors and marched one Sunday to the Congregational Church to join them in worship services. Originally adopted as "the Federated Congregational-Presbyterian Church of Hamilton," the name was later shortened to "The Hamilton Federated Church." The First Congregational Church purchased the present church site on February 5, 1879, for $200 from the Hannibal & St. Joseph

First Baptist Church (above). The old frame Baptist Church, built in 1876, suffered extensive damage by fire on Dec. 24, 1953. Trooper L. D. Jefferson was sitting in his car near the intersection of old highways 13 and 36 filling out a report when he heard glass breaking and saw smoke pouring from the building. A Christmas program had been held in the church on the previous evening and many gifts left by the congregation were destroyed. A new $70,000 brick church (inset) was dedicated on Sept. 26, 1954.

First Christian Church (above). Services were held in private homes until the $800 frame First Christian Church was completed in 1878. The building was located at today's site of the Church of Christ (inset)

RLDS Church. The Reorganized Church of Latter-Day Saints congregation purchased the old south side grade school at an auction in 1950, but after a fire destroyed the bell tower in 1967, plans were made to build another church on South Highway 13. The old south side school was torn down in 1981.

Apostolic Lighthouse Church. The Apostolic Lighthouse Church was founded in November of 2012 by Pastor Russell and Ruth Dotson, and Assistant Pastor Jeff and Rhonda Hurt, at 1009 South Hughes Street. Russell Dotson retired in June of 2014, with Jeff Hurt taking over the Pastorate. That building has undergone extensive remodeling to meet the needs of the growing congregation.

In February of 2021, the need arose for the church to have a new building. Property was purchased at 7835 North Highway 13 in July of that year. Construction of a new multipurpose facility, that would help meet the needs of youth in the community, was started in February of 2023 and the building was completed in April of 2024.

Apostolic Lighthouse Church is part of the United Pentecostal Church.

Sacred Heart Church. Sacred Heart Catholic Church was built in 1921 and remained a mission of Cameron until 1925. Earlier masses had been offered in private homes or in a rental hall by a Cameron resident priest. The earliest record of a mass in Hamilton dates back to 1859 when Father John Hogan, who would later become the first bishop of St. Joseph and Kansas City, offered it in the railroad depot.

Hamilton United Methodist Church. The Hamilton Methodist Life Center is attached to the older Hamilton Methodist Church (above). In addition to being the site of a modern praise and worship service each Sunday, the building has become a large community meeting and event venue.

24

COAL MINE HISTORY

Both the Caldwell Coal mine, east of the J. C. Penney farm, and the Tom Creek Coal Mine, southwest of Hamilton, were operating in the 1880s and through the 1930s.

Worker strikes were common, usually for higher wages. Miners then made between $2 and $3 per day. Most miners belonged to the Knights of Labor, which wielded some power. The first strike came in January 1886 at the Tom Creek mine. Col. J. W. Harper was mine superintendent and Frank Clark, the miller, was company president.

Miners at the Caldwell Coal mine followed suit and walked off the job. After several weeks, white strike breakers were brought in, but they were met at the train depot by the striking miners. This confrontation caused the strike breakers to leave in fear on the next train.

A second group of colored miners was brought in, and they remained for several years. In those days, striking employees rarely got to return to their jobs. Most miners lived in shacks near the mines, but the influx of colored miners no doubt led to an increase in the colored population in town.

In 1897 alone, the Caldwell Coal Co. mine produced 20,000 tons of coal with a shaft of 507 feet. Ventilation was provided by a 10 foot fan. The Tom Creek mine shipped for a time by the Hamilton & Kingston Railroad. The Caldwell mine had a spur to the Hannibal & St. Joseph tracks.

The East Coal Mine operated by Caldwell Coal Company

The Tom Creek Coal Mine operated until the beginning of the 20th Century

EARLY FIRES

Early Davis Street. This late 1883 or early 1884 photo of Davis Street looks north from today's site of The Hamilton Bank parking lot. The two brick buildings on either side of the street to the north are the Cash, Cowgill & Co. and Anderson buildings. Further up the street on the right side is the old three-story Phoenix Hotel. (Photo courtesy of Helen Thomson)

1883 Fire. The fire that destroyed nearly alll of the west-central block of Davis Street started in Lievan's Meat Market near the site of the Hamilton Hotel. The blaze swept away all the wood frame buildings up to the Cash, Cowgill & Co. brick building on the corner. (Photo courtesy of Helen Thomson)

1884 Fire. Townspeople were awakened on the morning of July 5, 1884, by a fire that wiped out nearly all the east-central block of Davis. Early fires played havoc with business life but led to bigger and better brick structures and more prosperous times for the town. (Photo courtesy of Helen Thomson)

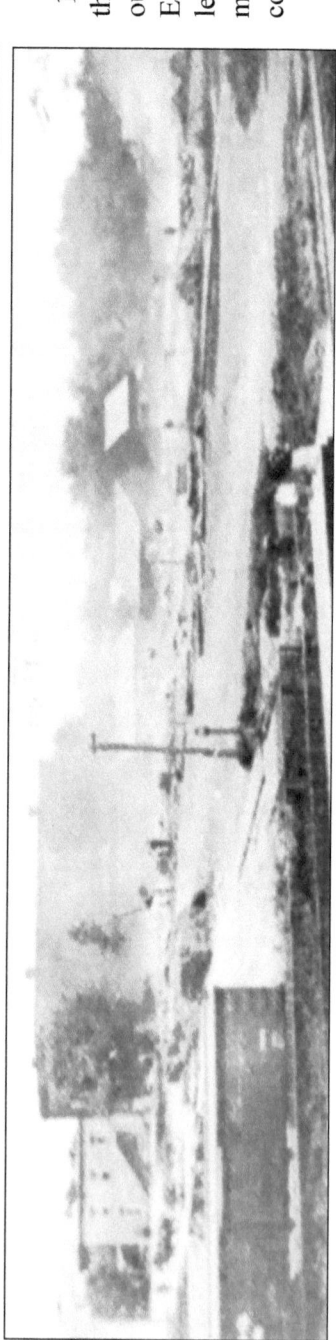

26

James O. Thornton. Born in Hamilton in 1868, Thornton began in the drug store business in 1885 as an apprentice to Rufus W. Napier. He went into partnership with his mentor in 1892 and continued in that capacity until 1894 when Napier retired. Thornton sold drugs, perfumes, cigars and tobacco, stationery and books. He eventually adopted the Rexall brand name and was the forerunner of French's Rexall and later Jim's Rexall. J. O. would turn the business over to his son, James E., upon retirement.

W. J. Ervin (1883-1921). Washington J. "Uncle Dick" Ervin (left) came to Hamilton in 1867 and opened the second drug store in town (above). He served with the Third Missouri Infantry of the Confederacy during the Civil War and was wounded in battle five times. He was a Hamilton druggist for 54 years but in his later years turned the business over to his son, Dr. W. E. Ervin.

Early Hamilton Businesses

H. L. BAINTER

Dray Businesses. Harve Bainter operated a coal and feed business, as well as a dray business (above) on North Davis on today's MFA Exchange site. Most dray men of the day operated some sort of business as well. The word "dray" was first used in the 14th century to mean a low, heavy horse cart used to haul freight or heavy loads. Other early Hamilton dray service operators were Fred Martin, Wes Hines, Archie Blades, L. T. Farr, M. E. Bolen, George and Edwin Gibson, Claude McBrayer, Walter Orr, Ray Hawks and George Boutwell.

Main Street Nutrition. The Main Street Nutrition building (2024) across the street north of the Penney Museum may be the oldest business building in Hamilton. In the 1860s it was the site of a brick factory started by A. G. Davis and operated by H. G. Hughes. William Stone built the present "iron clad" building in 1871 as an implement store. The building's covering was added by Mrs. Stone, who also cut off part of the east end of the building to make more room for her new home, which is now gone.

Early Livery. Above—Claude Campbell operated a livery stable sometime around the turn of the century, possibly the same one established by Sam McBrayer in 1898.

McBrayer livery. Upper left—Beginning around 1870 the McBrayer livery stable grew to be one of the centers of horse and mule trading and selling in the US. Run by Sam and his sons William and Sol, the livery stood where Dollar General stands today. The barn stabled as many as 300 animals with a blacksmith shop in the rear.

McBrayer Veterinary Hospital. Lower left—W. J. McBrayer operated a livery stable on South Davis Street and the accompanying hospital for horses and mules was across the street just south of today's City Hall. It burned on Dec. 27, 1937.

HAMILTON HOTELS

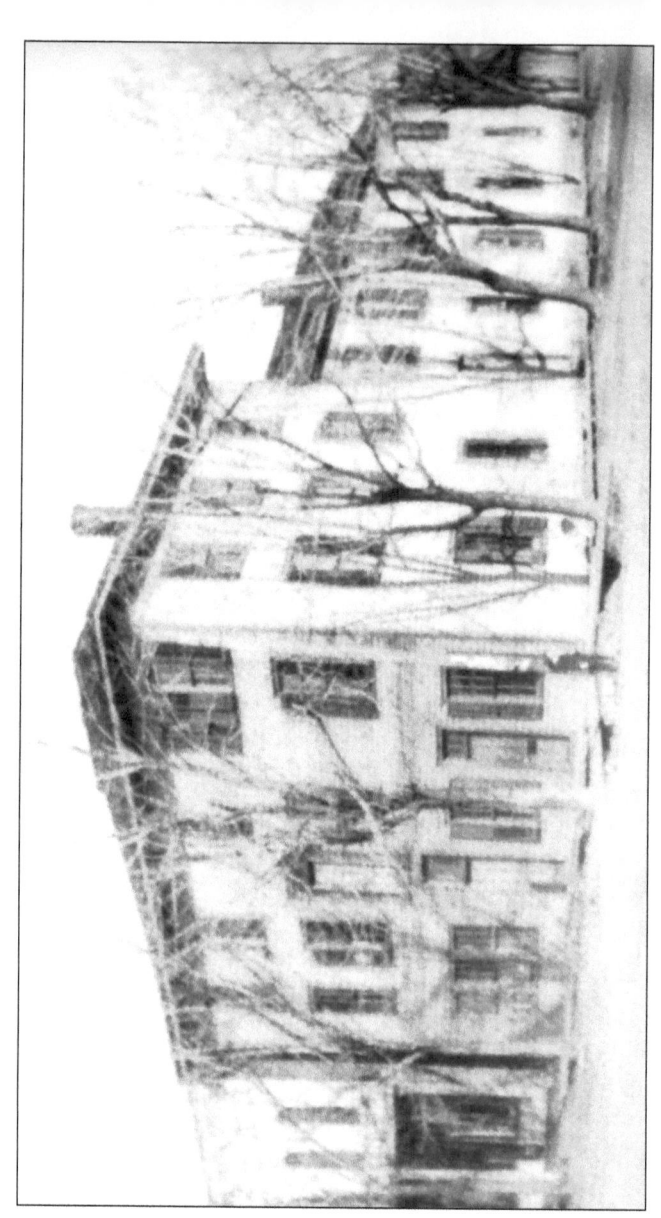

Savoy Hotel. Right–Originally the "Q" Hotel, it was built following the 1886 fire by Dr. Clayton Tirrin. The boarding house eventually sold to L. M. Battson in 1907, and he changed the name to the Savoy Hotel. A murder occurred in front of the hotel during the late 1890s. Missouri Star Quilt Company's headquarters now occupies the site.

Harry House Hotel. Below right–Mrs. C. Harry ran the Harry House Hotel during part of the 1870s and '80s. Built during the early 1870s as the Broadway Hotel, it was located at the corner of what were then known as Broadway and Mill Streets (now Ardginger and Berry). In its earliest days the hotel stood along the main route of the road from Gallatin to Kingston and beyond to Lexington. Ardinger was once considered the main street of town.

Mrs. Harry (below) was a widow when she ran the Harry House.

Train Depot. This turn-of-the-century view of the Hamilton Train Depot was probably taken from the roof of the Burlington Hotel on the east corner of Davis and McGaughy.

Steam locomotive. Above–An eastbound train passes through town. A modern looking Hotel dePorter stands in the background.

Train depot. (left–The Hannibal & St. Joseph train depot was completed in the fall of 1859. (Photo courtesy of Johnnie Henderson)

J. C. Penney—Hamilton's Famous Native Son

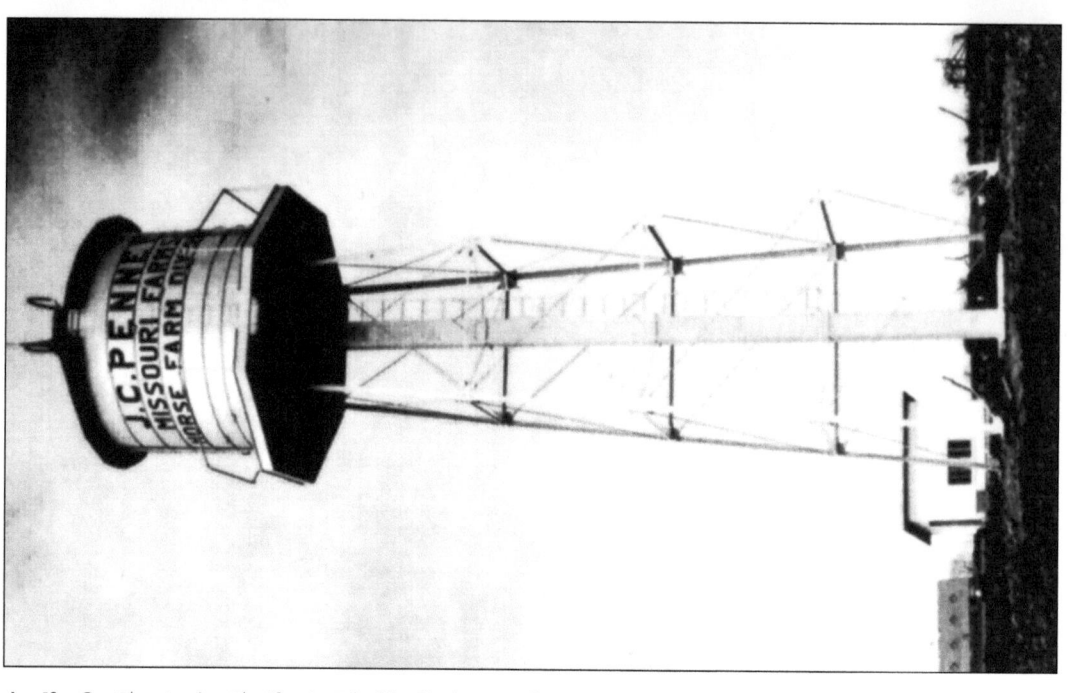

Hamilton, Missouri is the birthplace and hometown of J. C. Penney. That was once the town's biggest claim to fame, at least for outsiders who come to tour the Penney Museum and see his boyhood home that now stands on the site of the old railroad depot in the center of town.

The late retail magnate, who died in 1971 at age 95, maintained a close relationship with his hometown throughout his career.

James Cash Penney

Penney, born Sept. 16, 1875, in Hamilton, left here for health reasons and went West. He eventually established a chain of department stores across the nation and used the old-fashioned values he learned in Hamilton as a foundation of his business and personal life.

Hamilton definitely benefitted from his successful career. Penney opened the 500th JCPenney store here in 1924. He rented a house in town for his store managers but kept a room for himself and visited often. He also bought a farm east of town and made it an agricultural showplace during the Depression. He donated the town's first library, and helped ensure the building of a shoe factory, the high school, Highland Cemetery and the American Legion Park.

During J. C. Penney's lifetime, he refused to have any memorials established in Hamilton in his name. But today, Hamilton has a beautiful museum that also houses a public library and a well-used community room. Local groups and citizens maintained a strong relationship with Penney's newphew, E. R. "Bob" Penney, who had much to do with fund raising for the museum and for a trust fund established in the late 1980s to maintain the building. A portion of the street that runs by the boyhood home was even named for Bob Penney.

To help keep the Penney legacy alive today, the Hamilton Chamber of Commerce stages the J. C. Penney Days Festival each fall. Civic organizations also cooperate to encourage tourism and one of them, Second Century, helped oversee the moving of Penney's boyhood home to the Penney Park in the middle of town.

The Penney boyhood home, which was developed as a museum featuring furniture and household items typical of the time when J. C. Penney lived in the house, often is open to the public during special events.

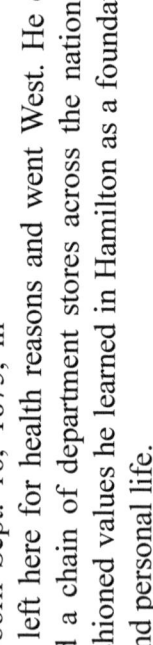

This tower was on the J. C. Penney farm east of Hamilton. Penney was well known throughout the country for his registered livestock.

Penney Building. The J. C. Penney Company store in Hamilton, the 500th store nationwide, opened in 1924. The building was the former home of the Hale-Goldsberry store and the J. M. Hale store before that. J. C. Penney worked in the J. M. Hale store before leaving to go West. He established his first retail store in Kemmerer, WY and called it The Golden Rule Store.

Inside former J. C. Penney store. Tin ceilings and hardwood floors were featured in early business houses. This shot of Hamilton's JCPenney store is looking from the rear to the front of the store.

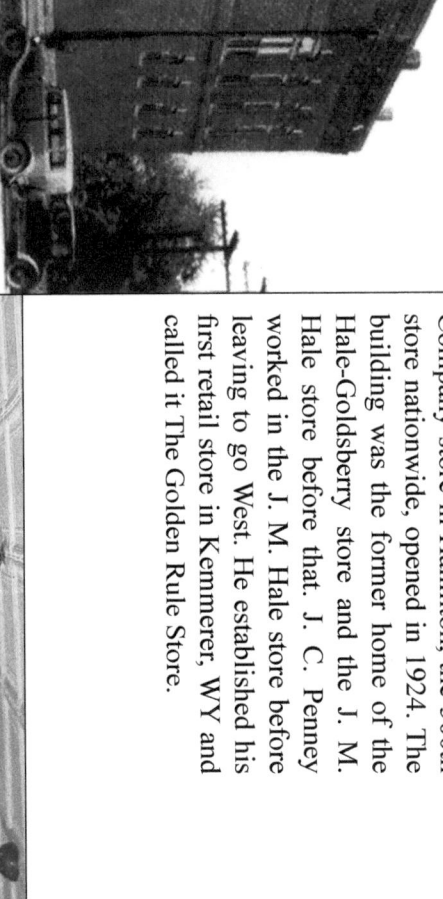

33

Penney Store Window. The Hamilton JC Penney store advertized back-to-school clothes for boys and young men, sometime during the 1940s. How about those prices?

34

A new horse and mule barn on the J. C. Penney farm east of Hamilton.

West side of North Davis. This early 1880s view looking north was taken from in front of the Anderson building and looks across the street toward the brick hardware building of John M. Morton. While John ran his hardware business in the south room of the building, his brother, William, was postmaster in the post office that took up most of the north room. Chalres Boroff ran a book store out of the post office.

East side of North Davis. This 1879 view looking north shows, from the right to left–the Houston, Spratt & Menefee Bank (the first brick building in Hamilton and the first bank in Caldwell County), E. H. Bishop's drug laboratory, G. L. McKenzie's boot and shoe store, George R. Rogers Drug Store and William Rhoades' New York Store (later the Phoenix Hotel).

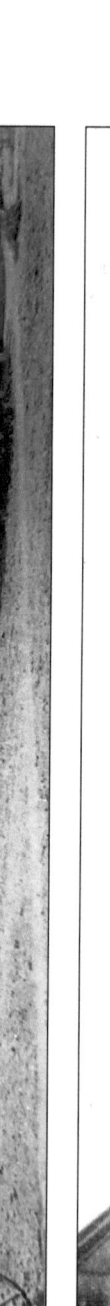

South Davis in 1882. Buggies and boardwalks are evident in this 19th century photo of South Davis Street. Looking north, the brick building on the right corresponds with the corner building at the stoplight. Across the street is the old Cash Mercantile building, with the Odd Fellows lodge upstairs. This building burned in the 1930s.

36

McBrayer Feed & Coal. Claude McBrayer was an enterprising man around the turn of the century and ran a coal and feed business out of the brick building just north of the railroad on Ardinger Street. At that time, his father, Sam, ran a livery across the street east on the present site of the Community Arts Theatre.

Moore Monument. George W. Moore opened his marble and granite monument shop and showroom in 1890 on South Broadway. Moore advertised monuments, tables, posts and "cemetery work of every description executed to order." Moore moved to Chillicothe in January of 1925, primarily for expanded shipping by railroad. Vince, son of George, retired from the family business in 1987 but his son, David, continued operating the business, which celebrated its 100th year. The piece of rough Missouri granite in the photo was cut for the George Rogers memorial and still stands by the north entrance of Highland Cemetery.

37

Anderson Building. The two-story, two-room brick building that stood on today's site of Hy-Klas Food & Family Center was built in 1872 by Anthony Rohrbough. It was the original site of the Kemper general store of the 1860s. W. W. Anderson looked after the mercantile business while his brother, Joseph, took care of a flourishing cattle business. The second floor of the building was used as an "opera house." The Freemasons also leased the upstairs in 1910. When the building sold to the Bram family in 1933, it was split into two separate rooms. The Brams established a funeral home in the south room with a separate street entrance. The north room was a hardware business. At the time of the 1965 fire, the building was vacant. Also destroyed in the fire were Western Auto, Dean Barnard's Tavern, Ben Bruce's Uptown Pool Hall and J. P. Jones' Variety Store. Fire companies from Hamilton, Gallatin, Cameron and Chillicothe fought the blaze.

1884 Street Scene. A saddle horse patiently waits out the rain at a hitching rail near the northeast corner of what is now Hy-Klas Food and Family Center. The one-story brick buildings across the street date this photo during the rebuilding period following the 1883 fire.

38

Frank Clark's Mill. The Hamilton Flour Mill, built in 1867 by John Sigman, thrived under the ownership of Frank Clark, who purchased his father's (Henry) interest in 1874. The mill was destroyed by a fire in 1878, but Clark immediately erected a three-story brick building with a basement. Patented roller mill equipment was added in 1892, making possible the sale of Legal Tender, White Loaf, Snow Flake and North Star–all excellent grades of flour. Clark added a dynamo in 1895 to turn steam power into electricity for the City of Hamilton.

Center Block of Davis St., East Side. This late 1800s photo shows, from left: Minger's Grocery & Bakery, S. H. Swarts (New Home Sewing Machines), A. C. Simpson Jeweler and an unknown drug store, possibly Baker's Drug. This is the current corner site of Missouri Star Quilt Company's Retreat Center.

Hobo Day. These young men spent a carefree day sometime around 1914 or 1915. Most of these "disreputable" characters were actually sons of some of the town fathers of that day. Included in the group were Dotty Lyons, Elton Eads. Lyle McAdo, Harry Thomson, Lamison Giddings, Jerome Ridings, Lile Arey and Sam McBrayer. (Photo courtesy of Darlene McIntosh)

The Hamilton & Kingston Railroad

Though little, if anything, remains to mark its passing, the railroad that once served Hamilton and Kingston had a proud beginning. Just nine miles in length, the Hamilton & Kingston Railroad filled an important need for the transportation of passengers, coal, goods and produce between the largest town in the county and the county seat.

The Haines, Hamilton & Kingston Railway Company was organized in 1890 to construct a standard gauge railroad from a point on the Hannibal & St. Joseph Railroad in the west end of Hamilton to Kingston. Local directors of the line were Frank Clark, Hiram Tilley, John N. Morton and D. G. McDonald, all of Hamilton, and S. C. Rogers and E. H. Johnson, Kingston.

The railroad bed was prepared in the summer of 1890, and by October, rail had been laid as far as the Tom Creek bridge. The engine arrived in Hamilton on October 15, and track was laid up to the west end of the Hamilton depot where a new 100-foot platform was built. A time card was issued by the H & St. Joe connecting Kingston trains with the passenger trains on the east-west line.

On Saturday, Nov. 29, the engine pulled out of the Hamilton station at 12:15 p.m. with two cars filled with people. A crowd of hundreds gathered at the Kingston depot for its arrival at 1 p.m. amid the boom of cannon, strains of music from the Kidder band and much shouting and flag waving. The depot at Kingston contained an engine house and stockyard and maintained a water tank on the north bank of Shoal Creek, with a windmill to lift water from the creek bed.

Passengers disembarking joined a parade to the Kingston Hotel for an elaborate celebratory banquet. Kingston mayor S. C. Rogers gave the address and Hamilton mayor B. M. Dilley provided the response.

The crowd marched back to the depot, where John D. Cox, a longtime county resident, drove the final spike, a silver one, into the rail. The train made it back to Hamilton about 4 p.m. after stopping along Tom Creek to pick up more passengers. Since there was no means to turn the engine around at Kingston, the train backed up all the way on the return trip.

Hamilton & Kingston railroad car. This old passenger coach from the Hamilton & Kingston Railroad rested for many years in a field east of the Kingston School, not far from the old Kingston depot. The coach carried passengers, mail, freight and other baggage from Hamilton to the county seat.

Business for the new rail line flourished for a time but it became difficult to meet expenses and to even keep the train on the tracks. Heavy rains constantly washed out bridge crossings and kept the rail bed in a deteriorated state. After a reorganization following bankruptcy, the line flourished again until around 1900 when it was finally abandoned. The rails were returned to the Burlington Railroad, from which they had been rented. The depot at Kingston stood for many years after the railroad's demise, but was finally razed.

HAMILTON PUBLIC SCHOOLS

Father of Hamilton schools. Professor David M. Ferguson was orphaned at age seven and attended school until age 16, when he began teaching in order to earn money for college. He came to Hamilton in 1868, not long after serving as an Ohio soldier in the Civil War. Upon taking over Hamilton schools in 1872, Ferguson immediately organized a "graded" system that plotted a specific course of study for each grade. He initiated Latin in the school curriculum and was responsible for holding "teacher institutes" in the summer that helped teachers get their teaching certificates. In addition to serving as head of Hamilton schools, he also served as Caldwell County School Superintendent.

Ferguson left Hamilton in 1882 for Paola, KS, where he taught before his death in 1912.

First public school building. In 1866, one year after the first public school was held in the second floor of John Morton's tinshop on North Davis, a one-story school building was constructed by a local carpenter on land purchased from the town company. The building, with a one-room addition, stood near the Methodist Church and was moved in 1876 to what was later the shoe factory parking. It served as the first south side grade school. It became known as the "Little Brown School" because it was painted brown when it was moved. South side classes were held there until 1887 when a new two-story brick building was erected. In later years, the frame building was moved to North Hughes Street, but it was eventually torn down.

EARLY BRICK SCHOOL BUILDINGS

When the north side Hamilton school (top) became overcrowded in 1876, the old frame school house, once located at today's site of the M. E. Church parking lot, was moved to what was later the shoe factory parking lot, for the benefit of south side students. It served until 1887 when a new two-story brick school was erected. Part of that wooden building was detached and served as the colored school and was located at the end of East Berry Street.

In the early 1900s, the Hamilton school district was told by the state that both north and south side buildings were outdated and should be abandoned. Both buildings were torn down in 1904-05 and during rebuilding, classes were held in empty stores, churches and upstairs in the J. M. Hale building, now the Penney quilt shop. This is when the outside stairs were added on the north side of the building.

Both new schools were completed in the fall of 1905. The south side school continued to serve grade school students through the 1940s. The south side building was eventually purchased by the RLDS church. It was torn down in 1981 after being abandoned for several years.

HIGH SCHOOL/ ELEMENTARY BUILDING

Early on the morning of Nov. 12, 1919, fire was discovered on the roof of the north side school building. Sparks from a chimney had ignited the roof, or a defective flue caused the roof to ignite. Teachers and students exited classrooms in an orderly fashion and no one was injured during the excitement.

An inspector from the State Department of Education had just visited the school and gave it an outstanding report.

High school classes were then held in the Baptist Church. Seventh and eighth grade classes, under Misses Stella Farabee and Helen Kautz, were held in the Rex Theatre rooms of the Hamilton Advertising Club (Ole Granary building). First through fourth grades, under Mrs. Frank McClelland and Miss Leta Gibson, met in the Christian Churh.

Following the fire, a bond issue of $35,000 was passed by Hamilton school patrons. Along with $13,000 insurance money, it was used to build a new high school building, which opened in 1920. This building today is the Missouri Star Quilt Museum.

44

Middle school groundbreaking. Hamilton R-II Board of Education members (from left) Bill Ford, Kathie Cornelius, Joe Sanderson, Earl Moore and president Rick Munroe broke ground on Oct. 10, 1990, for construction of a new middle school and gymnasium at Peney High School.

Penney High School groundbreaking and cornerstone ceremonies. Groundbreaking for the new Penney High School building took place on April 6, 1949, when L. G. Ehlers, president of the school board, lifted the first spade of dirt while J. P. Jones and M. O. Ridings of the board, R. E. Neale, superintendent; M. S. Dunham, principal; and members of the student body and faculty looked on. Masons were in charge of the cornerstone laying ceremony on Oct. 4, 1949. An afternoon parade to the new school site, and a night banquet at the Masonic hall were held with J. C. Penney in attendance. Over 1,200 attended the cornerstone ceremony.

Mr. Ehlers read a list of articles contained in a sealed copper box inside the PHS cornerstone. Some of the items inside the box were: a letter from Ehlers to future board members, a history of Hamilton schools by Dr. Bertha Booth, a copy of the revised Hamilton city ordinances, clippings from past copies of the Advocate-Hamiltonian and a copy of the 1949 Hamilton telephone directory.

Opening of the new school coincided with school reorganization into Hamilton R-2, and the closing and subsequent sale of 15 school houses, which resulted in the largest enrollment in Hamilton school history.

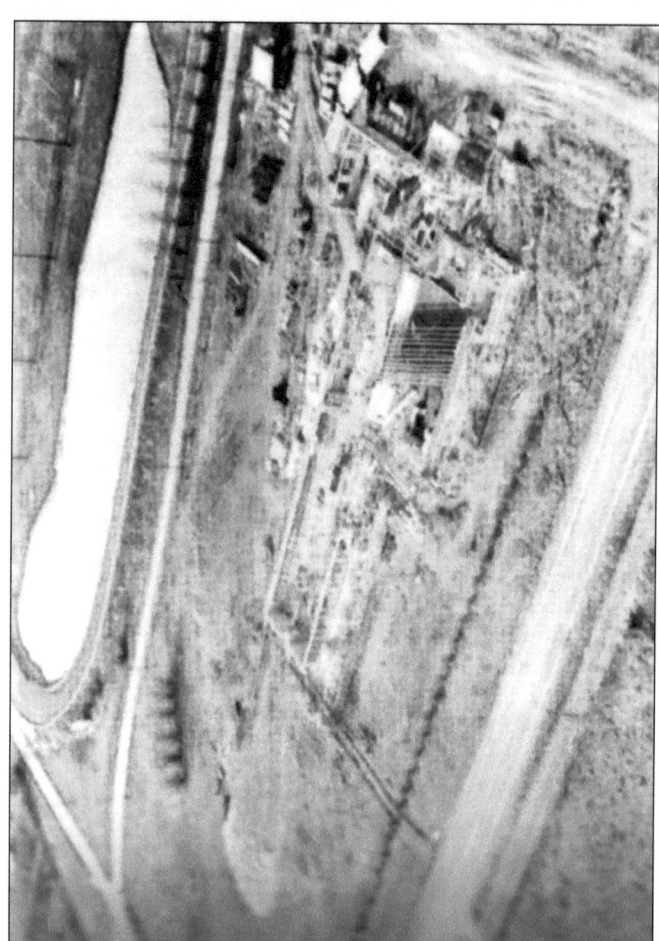

Penney High School Consruction. Above left and right–Penney High School construction began in the summer of 1949 and progressed quickly. J. C. Penney presented the board of education with 2,000 shares of common stock in the Penney Company, valued at $95,000, with the stipulation they be sold and the money used for construction of the school. Other members of the Penney family and former Penney employees combined for nearly $60,000 more in donations. Later, Penney gave an additional $17,500, which was to be matched by the community. More than 500 votes were cast on a bond proposal and special three-percent, one-year building tax levy and both passed by nearly 50 to 1 margins. One week after the election, the American Legion Post donated the south two-thirds of the Memorial Park grounds–eight acres total–to the school district as a site for the new school.

Completed PHS. A completed Penney High School (left) was ready for classes on Jan. 22, 1951.

46

Hamilton Elementary School. Hamilton R-2 School District placed a bond issue on the April 2007 ballot to raise funds to build a new elementary school north of the football field. Issues with the old building (now the MSQ Museum) were overcrowding, accessibility, electrical, heating and cooling issues within the building. The ballot issue was approved by 25 votes.

Under the direction of Steve Yost and the Board of Education, River Bluffs Architects were hired to finalize the design. Construction began on Oct. 2, 2007, with Straub Construction Co. having been awarded a $6.76 million bid.

When the new building was released to the district in February of 2009, head custodian Kenny Pulliam and crew took several trips moving classrooms from the old elementary building on Bird Street to the new location. Students and staff began school in the new building in August of 2009.

New Penney High School. Voters in the Hamilton R-2 School District overwhelmingly passed a bond issue (78%) to build a new Penney High School. Superintendent, Dr. Billie McGraw, and the Board of Education worked with Ellison-Auxier Architects of St. Joseph to finalize a design for the new school. As prices for construction continued to climb due to the effects of Covid-19, it was determined that by constructing the new high school in same place as the old school, it would reduce the square footage on the new construction, saving the district about $700,000. In August of 2022, a construction bid was awarded to Lehr Construction out of St. Joseph, to the tune of $8.535 million. High school students were able to attend classes during the 2022-23 term in locations around the community while construction of the new school progressed. On August 28, 2023, Penney High School students attended their first day of school in the brand new building.

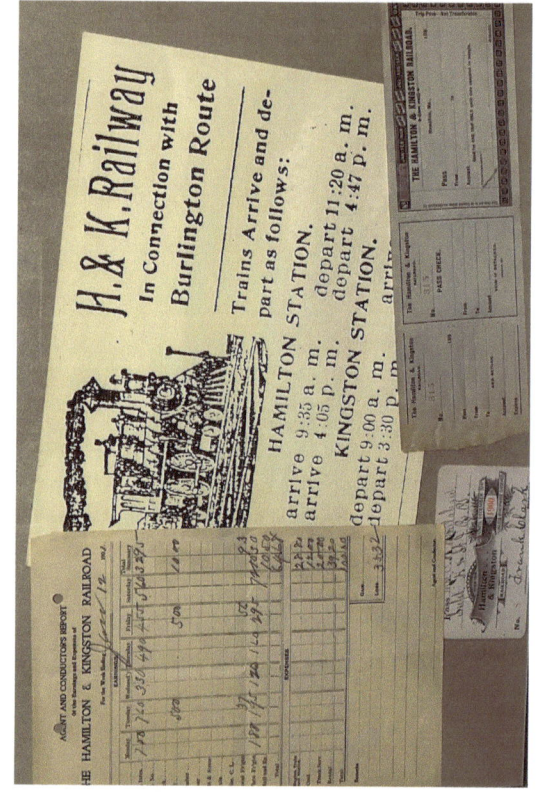

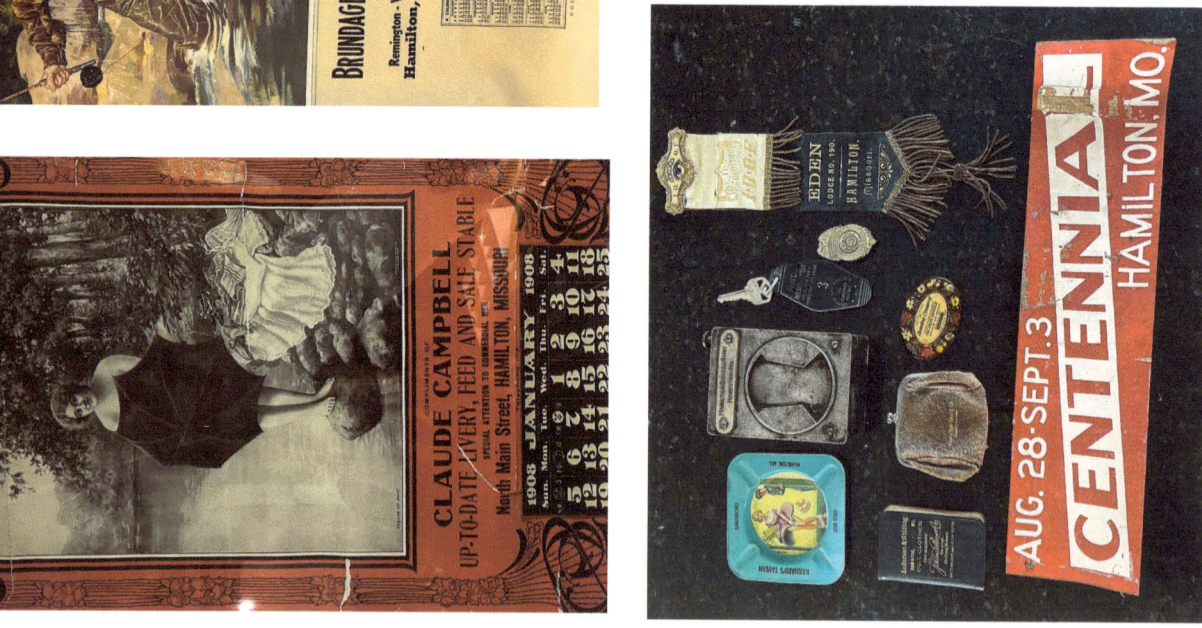

48

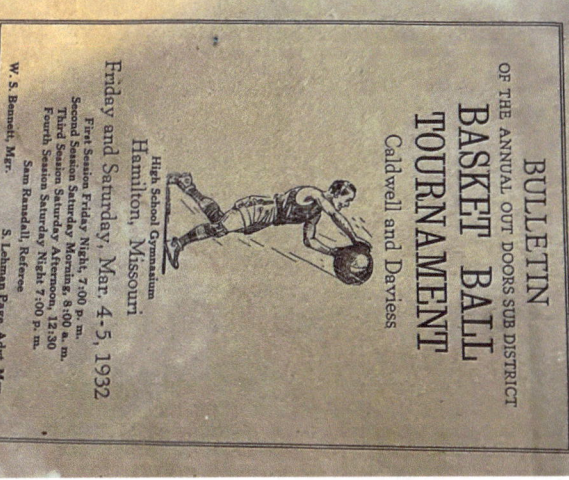

THE HAMILTONIAN.

CHRISTMAS NUMBER

HAPPY LAND

Happy land! Happy land! you come and join our band,
Blithe and gay, on the way
To Kris Kringle's Holiday?
Happy land! Happy land! you come and take our hand!
Merrily, cheer we go
To the Land of Gladness!
—BYRON WILLIAMS.

THE HAMILTONIAN.

HOLIDAY EDITION.

Volume XXVIII.   Hamilton, Caldwell County, Missouri, Thursday, December 21, 1905.   Number 2

All over the world
Every nation and clime
Let Santa Claus reign
At glad Christmas time

HAMILTON CELEBRATES 100 YEARS, 1855-1955

Citizens of Hamilton have seldom come together in spirit and with a greater sense of community pride than they did for the Hamilton Centennial Celebration in 1955. The celebration took months to prepare and hundreds of people volunteered to serve on the nearly three dozen committees formed in organizing the 100th year celebration.

Centennial week ran from Aug. 28 through Sept. 3 and featured a number of programs and performances. The Hamilton Centennial Choir performed throughout the week's events, which included the Parade of the Centuries on Davis Street, rededication of the restored historical marker by Cub Scouts and Brownies on the City Hall lawn, "Centurama" reenactment of the history of Hamilton, Old Settlers Day, Farmers Day and Great America Day. More than 300 women of all ages became Centennial Belles, and the "Brothers of the Brush" numbered nearly 150. More than 110 entries registered for the parade that drew an estimated 10,000 spectators and participants. President Dwight D. Eisenhower sent a telegram to the Hamilton Centennial Committee congratulating citizens of the town for their 100-year history. Former President Harry S. Truman provided a fitting climax to the final day of the celebration by delivering a speech on the Legion Park grounds.

CENTENNIAL FACTS & FIGURES

• Members of the Centennial planning committee were L. G. Ehlers, Sherman Henkins, G. O. Hunt, A. A. Miller, B. R. Denick, Roy Huey, L. R. Spainhower, C. A. Neal, L. O. Chadwick and Dale Oldfield.

• In April, Postmaster Roy Hendren announced that he had received over 500 requests for the Centennial postmark from people in 38 states, Canada, Alaska and the District of Columbia.

• In May, permission was granted by the city to erect a log cabin replica on Davis Street which would act as the official Centennial headquarters.

• Also in May, the schedule for the celebration was adopted. Sunday was named Church Observance Day. Monday was designated Parade Day. Tuesday was to be Youth Day. Wednesday was dedicated as Veterans Day. Friday was proclaimed Great America Day and Saturday was Industry and Agriculture Day.

• C. H. McIntosh was elected in June as president of the Brothers of the Brush, with Bob Hines as vice-president and P. A. Oldfield as secretary-treasurer.

• It was decided that the Saturday night activity would be a square dance, organized by Ross Hicklin, Harold Pierce, Gene Barnes and Owen Adams.

• By June, there were 283 members enrolled in the Centennial Belles and 78 members of the Brothers of the Brush.

• In July, it was announced that Dean Hales would be in charge of four nights of fireworks to be held at Legion Memorial Park.

• Charles N. Burrows, grandson of original town company member John H. Burrows, spoke at Sunday night's opening session.

• Marion Ridings, who published a special 64-page edition of the Advocate-Hamiltonian, received a congratulatory telegram to the citizens of Hamilton from President Dwight D. Eisenhower.

• The appearance of Harry and Bess Truman was said to have brought to town the biggest crowd in the history of Hamilton, plus an estimated 10,000 people turned out for the parade, which was two miles long and featured 110 entries. Some 250 workers at the International Shoe factory left their duties to march behind the shoe factory float.

• One of the features of the J. C. Penney Co. store float was a counter used by J. C. Penney in his first store in Kemmerer, Wyoming, in 1902.

• Estel Segar won the Centennial beard contest. Harriet Hawkins won the Centennial Belle contest for oldest dress at 115 years.

Krooked Kourt. Left–Oliver Hunt receives part of his punishment after appearing in Krooked Kourt during the 1955 Centennial celebration The Kourt was held at the corner of Bird and Davis Streets, near the post office, with Judge P. A. Oldfield presiding. "Ure Guiltee" (Bernard Potts) served as prosecutor and was opposed by L. O. Chadwick and J. P. Jones for the defense. Other cases heard involved charges against L. G. Ehlers, Glen Rogers and Alton Ruckman. Keystone Kops Harry Hawkins and Forrest Dixon administer punishment in the photo. Also serving as Kops were Junior Dunn, C. H. McIntosh and Fred Ford.

Centennial jail. Right–Serving sentences in the Krooked Kourt jail are, from left–L. G. Ehlers, Oliver Hunt, Alton Ruckman and Glenn Rogers. Kops on guard duty are Fred Ford and Forrest Dixon.

Log Cabin Replica. Left–Members of the veteran's ag class built the log cabin replica which stood near the Davis and Berry streets intersection. It served as Centennial headquarters.

52

Centennial queen (left). Carol Ann (Long) Lemery, daughter of Homer and Lucille Long, ruled over Hamilton's Centennial celebration during the summer of 1955. Her attendants were Mrs. Zona M. Dunn, and Judy Kleeman.

L. G. Ehlers was president of the Hamilton Centennial Corporation, formed as a steering committee for the events of Aug. 28-Sept. 3 of that year.

Other members of the board of directors were Sherman Henkins, L. O. Chadwick, C.A. Rouse, B. R. Demick, Roy Huey, G. O. Hunt, A. A. Miller, C.A. Neal, Dale Oldfield and L. R. Spainhower.

Centennial Belles. More than 300 Hamilton women of all ages joined the Centennial Belle organization for the 100th year anniversary celebration. The Belles, along with the Brothers of the Brush, inaugurated Centennial activities on June 18, 1955, with a Davis Street parade. The parade was just the first in a series of events in the formal observance of the town's Centennial. Pictured in the photo are Mrs. Edgar Burnett, Mrs. Walter Johnson, Mrs. J. P. Jones, Mrs. N. G. Hamlilton, Mrs. Roscoe Blackburn, Mrs. Leland Axon, Mrs. Connor Jones, Mrs. Roy Ogden and Mrs. Martin Abrahams.

53

AMERICAN LEGION RACE MEET HELD FROM 1932 TO 1950

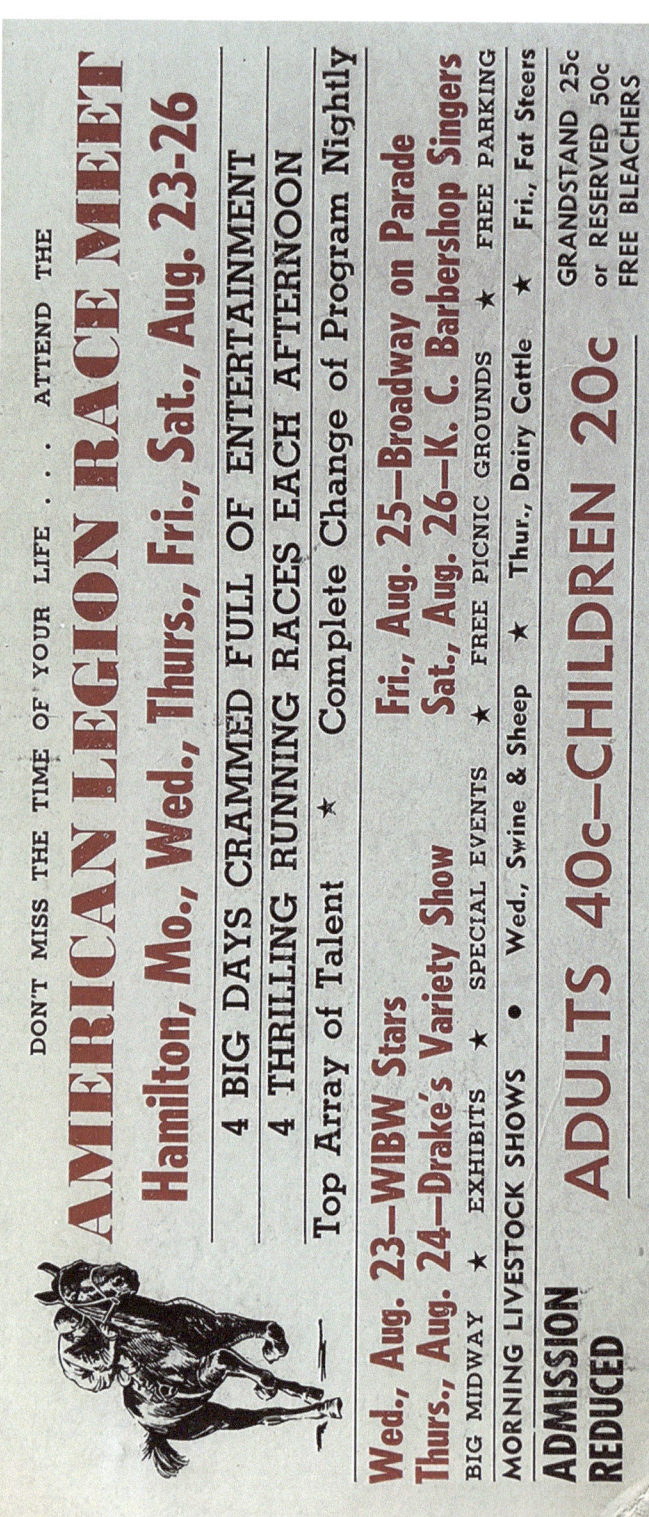

DON'T MISS THE TIME OF YOUR LIFE . . . ATTEND THE

AMERICAN LEGION RACE MEET

Hamilton, Mo., Wed., Thurs., Fri., Sat., Aug. 23-26

4 BIG DAYS CRAMMED FULL OF ENTERTAINMENT

4 THRILLING RUNNING RACES EACH AFTERNOON

Top Array of Talent ★ Complete Change of Program Nightly

Wed., Aug. 23—WIBW Stars   Fri., Aug. 25—Broadway on Parade

Thurs., Aug. 24—Drake's Variety Show   Sat., Aug. 26—K. C. Barbershop Singers

BIG MIDWAY ★ EXHIBITS ★ SPECIAL EVENTS ★ FREE PICNIC GROUNDS ★ FREE PARKING

MORNING LIVESTOCK SHOWS ● Wed., Swine & Sheep ★ Thur., Dairy Cattle ★ Fri., Fat Steers

ADMISSION REDUCED   **ADULTS 40c—CHILDREN 20c**

GRANDSTAND 25c
or RESERVED 50c
FREE BLEACHERS

Out of the gate: Horses and riders break out of the starting gate during the 1950 race meet. No races were held for two or three years during World War II.

54

Race Meet. Early race goers cross from the infield to the grandstand at the American Legion Race Meet.

Memorial Arch. The Hamilton Advertising Club met in the spring of 1919 to initiate a drive for funds to built a formal tribute to local soldiers and sailors returning from Europe after serving their country in World War I. It was decided that an arch would be erected on Davis Street, and club president C. A. Greene appointed J. F. Parrish, J. O. Thornton, J. E. Goldsberry and J. W. McLean to take charge of the project.

Plans were adopted for an arch 22 feet wide and 23 feet high. Judge Q. M. Kemper was put in charge of the construction crew. Mrs. Perry Roberts and Mrs. William Logan solicited funds from local businesses and individuals. The Memorial Arch was given to the North Missouri Fair Association in July of 1919, and it was moved to the southeast fairgrounds entrance. The arch was cut in two parts and extended so ten foot gates could be installed between ticket offices on each side. It is not known now when the arch disappeared.

Hamilton Stove Day - 1920

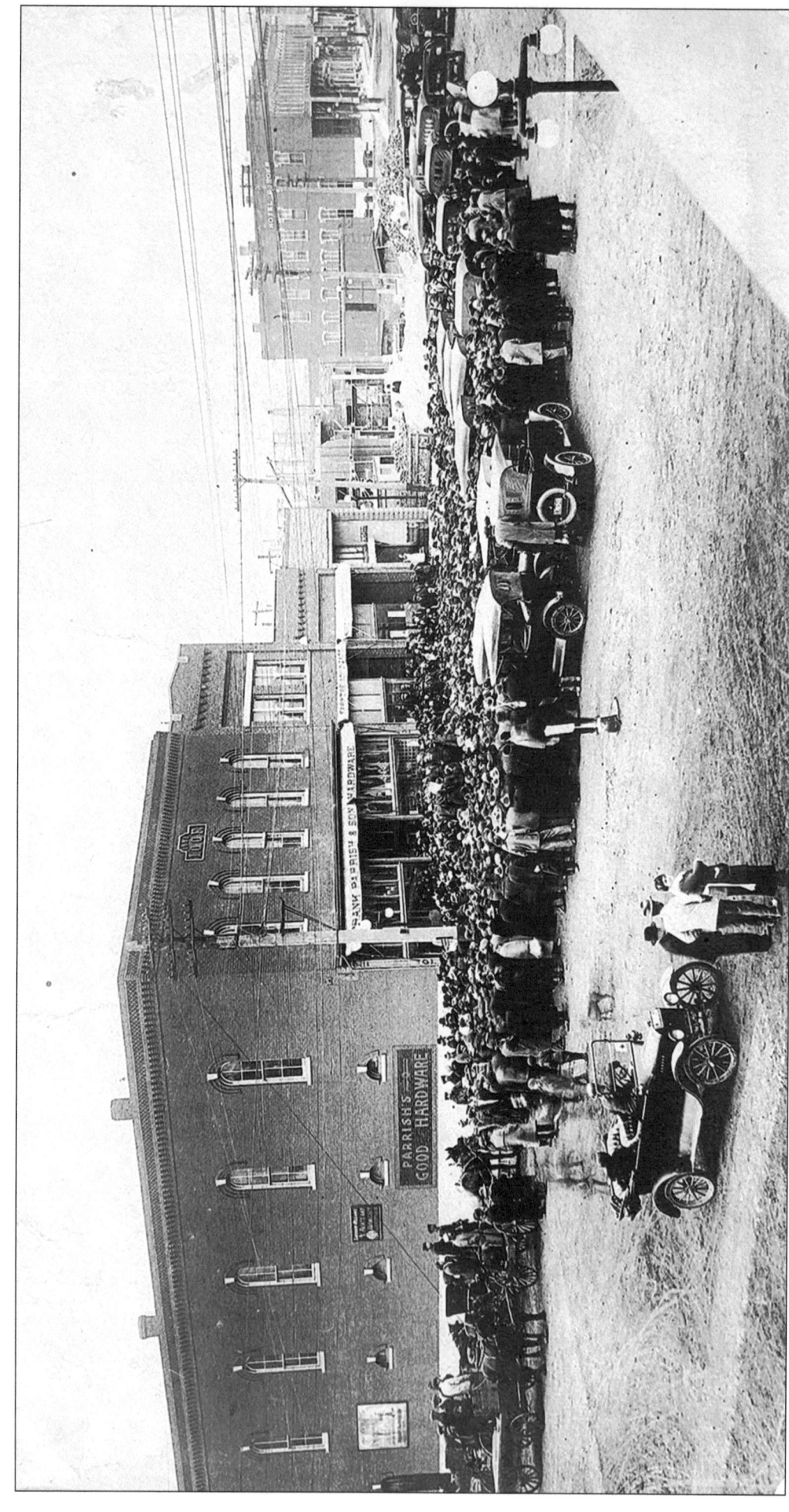

Hamilton had a bustling business district in the early part of the 20th Century. In those days Farnk Parrish & Son Hardware Store held a "Stove Day" drawing that drew a huge crowd for the chance to win a modern cooking stove.

56

Cash Mercantile. Top Right–Tire Day was the attraction in this 1928 photo of the Cash Mercantile Company's closeout sale. The building, located at the corner of Davis and Berry streets, housed the mercantile in the first floor and IOOC Lodge rooms upstairs. The building burned in January of 1937. The site was later the site of Harper Brothers Oil Co. Today the location is the site of Hamilton Family Health Center.

Martin Brothers Missouri Dry Goods building. Lower right–The Martin brothers learned the tin trade from Gideon Prentice, but Chet would go into the grocery business while Fina continued in the hardware trade. Chet operated this store in the north block of Davis Street, west side, until selling out to A. C. Menefee in 1898. He returned to the grocery business following a stint as cashier of the First National Bank. Chet retired from business life in 1934 after 52 years in business. Fina Martin's hardware store was located in the north block, east side. He tore down the old Phoenix Hotel in 1900 and erected a new two story brick building north of his store that would house the Missouri Dry Goods Co. in 1911. Partners in that venture were Fina's son, Donald, and C. A. Greene. In later years, this building housed the Gambles Store, run by Ross Hicklin, and later the Ole Granary restaurant run by the Thornton family. This photo also shows the Tiffin livery stable to the north, today's site of the J. C. Penney Museum.

C. A. "Chet" Martin came to Hamilton at age 19, along with his brother, F. A. "Fina" Martin.

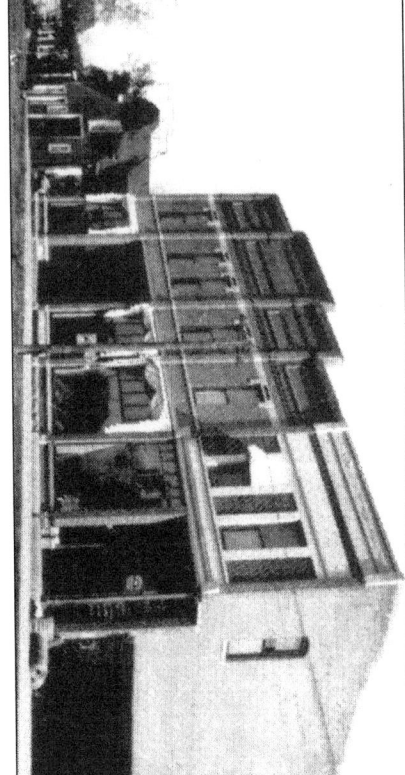

57

OLD FAIRGROUNDS NOW FOOTBALL STADIUM

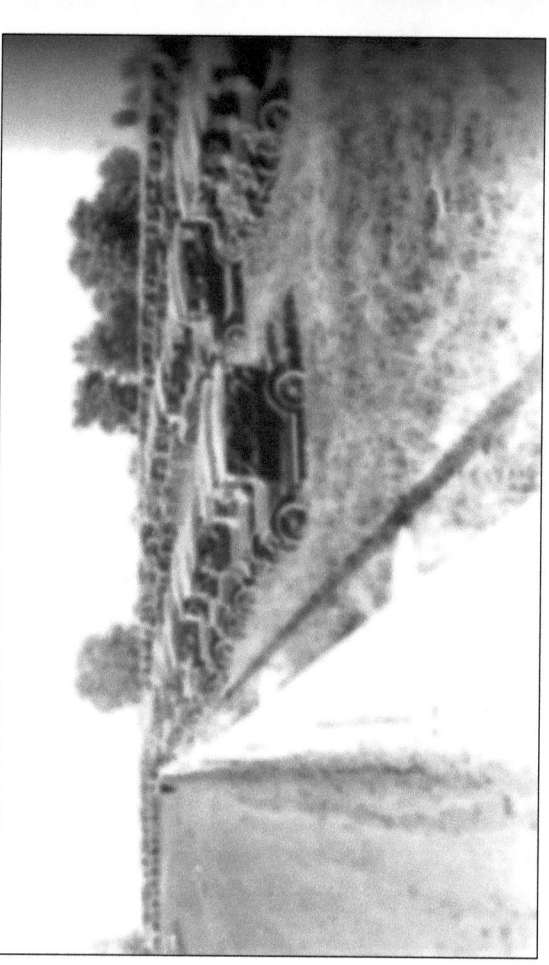

Hamilton Fair. The Hamilton District Fair, held 1883-1906, featured exhibits of farmers' produce, livestock, machinery and agricultural implements and lots of horse races. The event eventually gave way to the Hamilton Chautauqua.

Roaring Twenties parking. This photo, taken sometime during the early 1920s, shows cars parked along the rail of the half-mile race track on the Hamilton fairgrounds. The angle of the photo is looking northeast toward the present site of Penney High School.

Old fairgrounds grandstand. This is perhaps the oldest surviving photo ever taken of the fairgrounds during the time of the Hamilton District Fairs. This 1886 shot shows the old steeply-tiered grandstand and exhibition hall that stood about where the new concession stand is today north of the football stadium. Two barns can be seen in the background, along with numerous tents.

BUSINESS BUILDING FIRES IN 50s, 60s

1965 fire. Above, left–Five brick business buildings were destroyed and a sixth was badly damaged in the Aug. 22, 1965 fire on the east side of North Davis. Five fire companies fought the blaze for nearly four hours. Damage was estimated at $100,000. Among building destroyed were the vacant Bram building, Russell Bretz's Western Auto, Dean Barnard's Tavern, Ben Bruce's uptown Pool Hall and J. P. Jones's Hamilton Variety Store.

1966 fire. Above–Fire broke out around 4:20 p.m. on Aug. 13, 1966, in the second floor of the Humphrey bilding in the north block of Davis Street. Destroyed were Humphrey Plumbing and Heating, Real Gas Corporation, Ray Thomson's Appliance Center, Orville Gooding's B. and M. Doughnut Shop, the Missouri Power and LIght Co. office, M. U. McCrary's MFA Insurance Agency and Hill and McCrary Realty.

Variety store fire. Left–A fire in May of 1952 completely destroyed the stock of J. P. Jones's Variety Store in the east center block of Davis Street. The fire started from a burning trash pile in the rear of the City Food Market next door to Minger's Fountain and Grill.

Thomson Hardware. Probably no man in Hamilton was better trained for business than Guy Thomson, center of photo. He was one of Hamilton's most prominent businessmen for more than 70 years. He began in 1890 at the age of 18 with the J. F. Colby & Co. lumber and mercantile business and later worked for Gideon Prentice, who himself received early training in the tin and hardware trade from John M. Morton. Thomson worked for Fina Martin from 1893 until Martin's death in 1924 and then stayed on with Donald Martin, and later, McMaster Hardware. Thomson purchased the business from McMaster in 1938 and was later succeeded by his son, M. E. Thomson.

Pictured in the photo, taken in 1944, are Harry Thomson, Sr., M. E. Thomson, Guy, Les "Marquand" Baird and Ray Thomson. The dog, named Major, belonged to Harry.

Hales Market Trio. Inside Hales Market are Dean Hales, Junior Hollingsworth and Dean Davis.

60

School crossing guard. (Right) In rain, snow or fair weather, Mr. McQueen was always in his position in the middle of West Berry to help south side school kids cross the street. McQueen lived in the house in the background, a two-story house, once the home of Mrs. Littleton Gregory.

Commercial Club. A forerunner of the Chamber of Commerce, the Commercial Club held its meeting in the large hall above the Missouri Dry Goods Store (Thornton's Ole Granary)

Members of the men's class of the Federated Church in 1931 included, front row, from left–True D. Parr, P. B. Cole, Chet Martin, Dr. J. G. Bouaum, Prof. Bennett, C. A. Dovenspike, George Gibson, Seth Young, Dr. Lee Smith and Charles Anderson. Back rwo, from left–Loyd Roberts, Dr. Lyle Guffey, Elmer E. Clark, I. A. Frost, John H. Cowley, Rev. Clarence Almon and C. F. Ridings.

62

Standard Service Station. The site of the Standard Oil Company was originally the residence of Robert Houston, the banker, in the 1870s. He sold his cottage to Judge Dodge, who moved it off the site and built the house that stood south of Clifford Scott's State Farm Insurance lot. The filling station was built in 1928 and was first operated by George Sturgis. Pictured here are Lewis Gregory, Charley Gregory, Junior "Speed" Hollingsworth and an unknown highway patrolman.

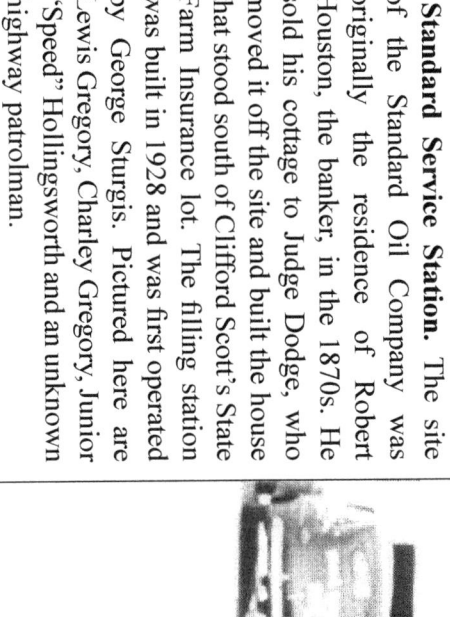

63

Missouri Power & Light Crew. The Missouri Power & Light crew, from left: Don Norris, Cleaburn Cook, Ben Woody, Bill Jack Jordan, Jim Akey and Ralph Blades. Photo circa 1968.

History of Hamilton Banking

A. C. Cochran established the first bank in Hamilton; in fact, the first bank in Caldwell County, in 1868. Robert Houston and John Spratt took over the bank in the early 1870s and soon added A. C. Menefee as a third partner. The Houston, Spratt and Menefee Bank remained in business until the 1890s.

The Hamilton Savings Bank was organized in 1878 with Crosby Johnson as president and Dan Booth as cashier. In 1889, Booth was named president of the newly-formed First National Bank of Hamilton. The Hamilton Trust Company was formed in 1916 through consolidation of the Hamilton Savings Bank and the short-lived Farmers and Merchants Bank. It was later succeeded by The Citizens Trust Company. A new building was erected for the First National Bank in June of 1920, and that building was gutted by a fire in January of 1929 but then quickly remodeled.

A merger of the First National Bank and The Citizens Trust Company in 1930 established the First Bank and Trust Company in the building formerly occupied by First National. True D. Parr was president and C. A. Dovenspike served as vice-president. Also on the board were M. E. Overstreet, Frank L. Bowman, Walter I. Hemry, Crosby C. Johnson, Jr., C. H. Lampton and Dr. Herbert R. Booth.

The Hamilton Bank opened its doors on June 11, 1938, after an 11-month absence of banking in Hamilton due to the closing of the First Bank and Trust Company in the later years of the Great Depression. L. G. Ehlers was president of the new bank, Elmer E. Clark was vice-president, H. M. Zook served as cashier and Marian Bretz was bookkeeper. Raymond Hartley and M. Fern Ehlers sat on the board of directors.

Ned L. Snyder began as a bookkeeper for The Hamilton Bank in 1946 and was named president in January of 1966. In 1969 he took over as chief executive officer upon the death of L. G. Ehlers. Ned's son, Larry, began with the bank in February of 1973 and became chief executive officer upon his father's retirement in in 1988. Larry stepped down from daily operations in 2012 but remained as chairman of the board

until 2021. Daughter Jessica Snyder Green took his place as CEO. The Hamilton Bank opened a Breckenridge facility in May of 1975. The Kingston Bank was formed in August of 1947 after voluntary closure of The First National Bank of Cowgill. Cramer Clark was named president of The Kingston Bank, A. E. Otto and W. D. McNary served as vice-presidents and Earl W. Carwford was cashier. When the bank built a new main facility in Hamilton in 1985, its name was officially changed to Caldwell County Bank and later to Bank Northwest.

First National Bank. Sitting on today's site of The Hamilton Bank, the First National Bank of Hamilton was established in 1889.

Dan Booth. Dan Booth brought his family to the Lovely Ridge area west of Hamilton in 1873 and took up farming and cattle raising before moving to Hamilton in 1881 and becoming cashier at the old Hamilton Savings Bank. Later he would become associated with The First National Bank and served as its president from 1898 to 1920, when he became president of the board of directors, a position he held for the rest of his life. Before coming to Missouri, Dan Booth served two terms as sheriff in Vinton County, Ohio. Both The First National Bank and Citizens Trust Company in town closed for his funeral in 1924.

Hamilton Savings Bank. These "graybeards" acted the part of holdup victims for the photographer in front of the Hamilton Savings Bank sometime around the turn of the century.

Bank opening. The Hamilton Bank opened June 11, 1938 under president L. G. Ehlers. Pictured on opening day are, from left, two out-of-town couples, Fern Ehlers, Mrs. H. M. Zook, L. G.Ehlers, Marion Bretz Borgmier, Erma Ehlers Snyder, G. F. Guiberson, Mrs. J.T. Baxter, Mrs. Lettie Ivie and Mrs. Guiberson.

The First National Bank and The Hamilton Bank. The old First National Bank building was razed in 1920 and replaced by this building, which was badly damaged in 1929. Fire gutted the structure but the bank vaults and safety deposit boxes were unharmed. The fire was thought to have started in the furnace room near the southwest corner of the basement and somehow jumped past the first floor to the upper story. The large columns in the lobby acted as flues which carried the flames to the second floor, which housed offices of Dr. J. B. Savell, dentist, and Dr. Herbert Booth. The building was remodeled and served as headquarters for The Hamilton Bank until the late Twentieth Century, when it was given a "facelift". While it still has a second story conference room and storage, all the offices are now on the ground level.

Bank Northwest. The Kingston Bank opened in July of 1947 and a branch was opened in Hamilton in 1985. The Farmers Bank of Polo was acquired by the Caldwell County Bank in 1993, when the bank's name was changed to Bank Northwest. Bank Northwest operates branched in Hamilton, Cameron, Bethany, Stanberry and Polo.

Till/Kavanaugh fire. An overheated chimney in the north room of the Kavanaugh Motor Co. building started a roof fire resulting in the total destruction of that building and the Artilla (Till) Theatre on North Ardinger on Feb. 3, 1949. E. C. Francis and Ina Faye Trosper Kavanaugh were part owners of the Oldsmobile and GMC truck dealership. Harry Till owned the theater since 1943, having purchased it from J. E. Courter of Gallatin.

Till Theatre Reopening. The Till (or Artilla as it was sometimes known) reopened in June of 1949 after the devastating fire that started in the Kavanaugh Motor Company building to the north. Harry Till first leased, then bought the theater from J. E. Courter of Gallatin in 1943. It was known as the Plaza Theatre in the 1930s, McBrayer Theatre for some years in the 1920s and the Rex Theatre in 1920 and perhaps earlier. Another theater, the Airdome, operated outdoors in good weather at the same time as the Rex. It was located one block east of Davis Street on McGaughy.

67

Hamilton Truck & Tractor Co. John Watson brought his International Harvester busines to Hamilton from Nettleton during the late 1930s and in 1945 he was bought out by his brother-in-law, Leslie Hines. Hines operated the business with his son, Robert, from 1946 until his death in 1972. Bob carried on for a year and then closed. The Hineses sold Plymouth and DeSoto automobiles from 1946-56 and in 1957 changed to ITCO and Massey Ferguson. They later added GMC trucks to their line. The present building was erected by Ezra Cope in the 1920s. Fred Graer operated a blacksmith shop here for more than 30 years until 1900. R. H. Pawsey operated ITCO at this location through the 1990s.

West Side Machine Shop. Claude McBrayer operated a coal and feed business at this site in the first decade of the 1900s. H. D. Skinner bought the building in 1918 and sold a variety of farm implements, including cream separators, hog oilers, walking and sulky plows, metal chicken coops, Klondike incubators, Emerson buggies, corn binders, manure spreaders, planters, cultivators, and for the home, Copper Clad ranges.

For nearly 100 years this building has been the site of a machine shop. The current owner is Ed Ernat. Previous owners were Clarence McCutchan and Harry Muller.

This photo, taken atop the JCPenney store building, shows the R. J. A. Bram Hardware and Undertaking business in the old Anderson building. The firm had just received a shipment of "new" Maytag ringer-type washing machines.

69

Hawks Motor Company. Fred Hawks founded Hawks Motor Company in 1910. The new building and Hawks Service Station, later Drumm Oil, were occupied in 1920. B. A. "Bud" Hawks went into partnership with his father in 1926 at a branch garage in Breckenridge. In 1929, Hawks motor discontinued Ford line and switched to Chevrolet.

Pictured in the photo below are: Fred, Bessie Rigdon, bookkeeper from 1921 until her death in 1953; Dean Rigdon, body man; and Bud.

Following Bud Hawk's retirement, John Sharp, and later his son, Doug, operated the Chevy dealership (above). Dale Scott was the last owner of the dealership before it closed in 1998.

70

City Hall and fire truck. In 1911 Hamilton voters approved $5,000 in bonds for construction of a city hall, shown in the background. The site was purchased from the town company in 1862 by Enos Dudley, and in 1863 the Hamilton House Hotel was built. It served the town until 1886, when it burned. To the east of the hotel, near the rear of today's Hamilton Bank, was the old News-Graphic print shop.

Boutwell Truck Service. George Boutwell ran a coal and transfer business in a brick building that used to adjoin the back of the theater on Ardinger Street. Phil Muller operated a coal office there in the 1920s and '30s before renting to Boutwell. E. C. Kavanaugh bought the site in the 1940s and ran his salvage and auto parts business there. Boutwell moved to the site of the old Moore Monument company on South Ardinger.

Barrel stave factory. Left–This factory that made staves for wooden barrel construction was in business during the 1880s on the site of the Community Arts Theatre.

Colby Mercantile Co. Below, left–This was the original office building of the Colby Mercantile Company when it opened at the corner of Berry and Colby Streets. Up until the time of Hamilton Supply, there had always been a lumberyard on this site. J. F. Harper started the business in the 1870s but sold to J. F. Colby in 1889. In time Colby bought all the holdings of the McBrayer Livery to the south and built the business into one of the largest lumberyards in the state. At the death of William F. Colby, the yard was bought by the Ballew Lumber co. of Kansas City. Sherman Henkins ran the Hamilton Lumber Company here for many years.

The young men's Sunday School class of the Methodist Church posed with their moms on Mother's Day in 1927.

73

Shaney Motor Company. Shaney Motor Co. started out in Nettleton before moving west of Hamilton on Old Highway 36. The firm contracted at one time to sell Oldsmobile and Volkswagen automobiles.

Imperial Service Station. The Imperial Station was on North Davis at the corner with Samuel Street. It is now the site of Kathy's Kitchen.

Ray Everett Motors shows off the 1949 Car of the Year, a Chevrolet, on the showroom floor.

74

Memorial Park Lake. Also called Chautauqua Lake at one time, the pond on the old fairgrounds was once a fair-sized body of water. The pond was drained in the late 1940s or early 60s when it became a breeding ground for mosquitoes. When the dam was breeched in the draining process, the entire area around today's municipal swimming pool was flooded. This view of the lake looks northwest across what is now the site of the Penney High School track.

Race Horse. Always a popular sport in early Hamilton, horse racing reached its height of popularity in the 1930s. This 1890s photo of unknown horse and rider was taken by Hamilton photographer T. H. Hare in the alley close to what would later be the site of the Hamilton Public Library. The depot and the back end of the Hamilton Hotel is visible in the background.

Livestock barn. Cattle, swine, sheep and poultry were judged during the four-day North Missouri Fair first held in Hamilton in 1919. Col. F. E. Williams was placed in charge of work crews constructing a new 120' x 36' hog and sheep barn.

75

Historic Hamilton Homes

101 N. Gallatin
Joseph Anderson
1904

310 E. Samuel
Dr. W. T. Lindley
1896

112 S. Ardinger
Crosby Johnson
1889

305 N. Gallatin
W. W. Koonse
1914

301 W. School
Dr. Will Alpin
1890

213 N. California
Irene Austin
1890s

306 E. Berry
J. M. Hale
1893

411 W. Berry
Col. J. W. Harper
1892

1029 S. Hughes
Edward Kennedy
1914

408 E. Ewing
Hiram Tilley
1890

308 S. Hughes
George W. Moore
1894

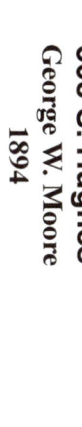

200 E. Berry
Roy White
1910

204 E. Berry
Elmer E. Clark
1892

409 N. Ewing
George Crockett
1903

300 N. Prairie
A. G. Davis
1875

207 S. Hughes
John Tippit
1900

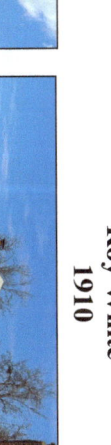

211 E. Samuel
P. A. Switzer
1920

201 E. Berry
(Gone)
Chet Martin
1899

302 E. Berry
Stephen Scott
1880s

77

HAMILTON HAS A RICH NEWSPAPER HISTORY

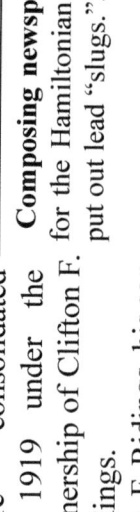

The Hamilton Investigator, published by Gabe Paxton and J. M. Gallamore, was established in 1867, and Paxton later sold his interest to Ben Whitely, and the plant was moved to a frame building east of the old city park. Whitley sold his interest in 1870 to M. A. Low and the name of the paper was changed to the *Hamilton News*.

The plant was then moved to the east side of south Davis when the Low-Gallamore partnership was dissolved. Low continued to run the *Hamilton News* for a number of years with B. M. Dilley as local editor. Low sold the paper to James Hitt and he first had John Marens as a partner, then Gus Chapman. Mr. Chapman soon tired of the newspaper business after he and Hitt established the *Graphic*. Chapman sold to Marens and the new firm acquired the *Hamilton News* and christened their new paper, the *News-Graphic*, in 1877.

In 1878, William A. Morton established the *Hamiltonian* and ran it until 1887 when W. J. Clark became publisher and editor. James Barnhill established *The Farmers Advocate* in 1890 and it was later bought by Al Filson. *The News-Graphic* was absorbed by the Farmers Advocate and all Hamilton papers were consolidated in 1919 under the ownership of Clifton F. Ridings.

C. F. Ridings, his son, Marion O. and grandson John, ran the *Advocate-Hamiltonian* until 1983, when Anne Chadwick purchased the paper and it became *The Hamilton Advocate*.

During the tenure of the Ridings family, two Kingston papers were brought into the publishing firm–*The Kingston News* in 1921 and *Caldwell County News* in 1953. *The Breckenridge Bulletin*, also owned for a time by M. O. Ridings, was consolidated in 1983 with the Advocate. Anne continued to publish the Advocate and in 1987 bought *The Braymer Bee*. Both papers were consolidated in 2005 into a new *Caldwell County News*.

Steve and Stephanie Henry purchased the paper in 2013 and continued to publish it in 2024.

Composing newspapers. Two linotype operators for the Hamiltonian type on machines that would put out lead "slugs.".

South Davis in the 1880s. On the second floor was the News-Graphic and T. H. Hare Studio. On the first floor L. A. Engle Drug and A. G. Howard Drug, were located on the former site of The Hamilton Advocate.

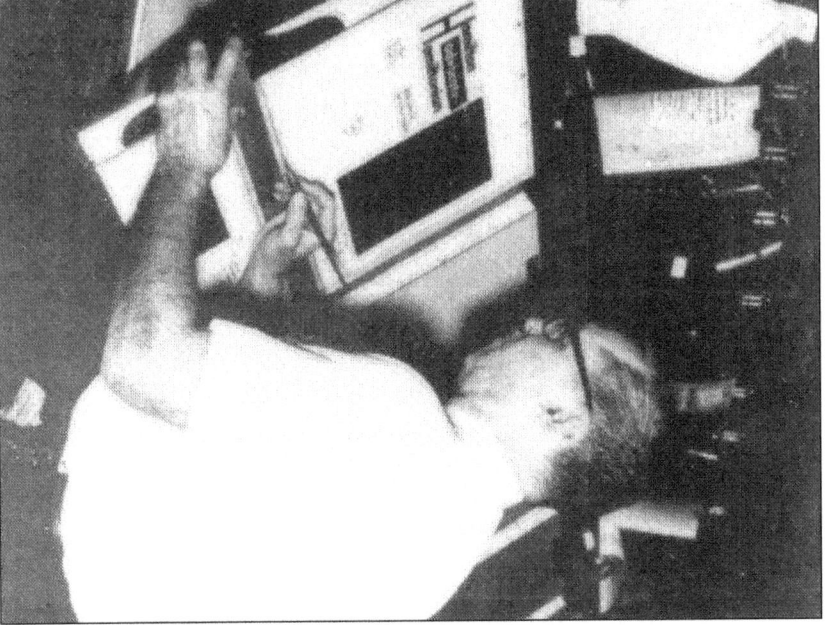

Dueling Editors. W. J. Clark of the *Hamiltonian*, and Al Filson of the *Farmers Advocate* didn't get along. The two men clashed often and verbally in their newspapers over politics and subjects such as electric lights and railroad issues. In 1890, Clark accused Democrats of holding back enterprise and new ideas. He also implied that Democrats could have saved the expense of having an election by not nominating anyone. While more subdued in tone, Filson challenged the existing order of the day while coming out on the side of farmers and labor unions. The feud often carried over to other towns. For instance, Filson had the *Gallatin Democrat* in his corner while Clark was cozy with the *Gallatin North Missourian*.

M. O. Ridings. Marion Ridings worked at the family newspaper through high school and college, and took over active management of the *Advocate-Hamiltonian* in 1941. His father, C. F. Ridings, purchased the *Farmer's Advocate* in 1900 and consolidated that paper and *The Hamiltonian* in 1919. M. O. published Hamillton's only newspaper until 1983.

79

View on Main St. Hamilton, Mo.

Just an average Davis Street gathering for one of Frank Parrish's famous Stove Day drawings. Held each fall from 1903 to 1927, Parrish Hardware drawings featured a giveaway prize of the latest model kitchen stove.

Paving Davis Street. In January of 1926, Hamilton aldermen passed a resolution to pave five blocks of Davis Street, from the Congregational Church north to the old Paxton Brothers livery barn (corner of old Imperial Service Station). The firm of DeJarnett & Schrader of Sedalia got the job with a low bid of $32,307. The reinforced concrete was laid down seven inches thick, and provision was made to continue the diagonal center parking for automobiles. The city council later cooperated with the State Highway Commission in paving Mill (Berry) Street from Dr. Tinsley Brown's residence east to the old Frank Clark Mill corner. Workers used a steel wheel tractor to prepare the grade for paving in front of Cook's Market and Parrish Hardware.

Late 1940s or early 1950s aerial photo of downtown Hamilton. Notice the parked cars in the middle of Main Street; something the town was famous for.

82

319 S. Hughes
Q. M. Kemper
1923

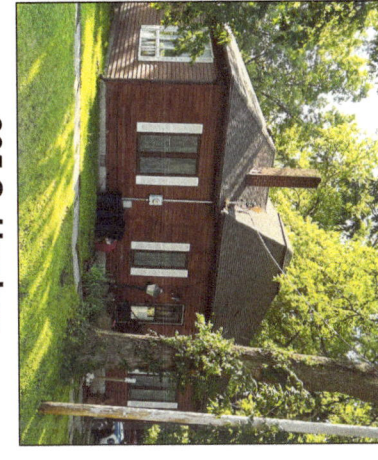

305 S. Hughes
Charles Walrath
Before 1915

401 N. Gallatin
William Altman
1908

407 N. Gallatin
W. H. Toon
Before 1906

1022 S. Hughes
A. F. French
Before 1908

410 S. Hughes
F. Eugene Morris
1911

608 S. Hughes
E. E. Henry
Before 1910

1014 S. Hughes
R. C. Porter
1908

202 S. Frame
J. R. Cheshire
Before 1910

407 S. Hughes
Ezra Ballard
1914

83

209 S. Hughes
Jackson Edminister
1904

207 N. Ardinger
James O. Thornton
1897

311 S. Ardinger
Dr. Lyman Brown
1894

409 N. Burruss
E. L. Cutbirth
1910

515 E. Arthur
F. A. Martin
1892

107 S. Ardinger
Mabel White
1915

409 E. Arthur
James Whitt
Before 1892

211 E. McGaughy
M. C. Martin
Before 1905

705 N. Davis
W. J. McBrayer
1903

84

101 W. Berry

Dr. Tinsley Brown

1909

307 N. Ardinger

Presbyterian Parsonage

1896

501 W. Berry

F. J. Bauer

1916

501 E. Sixth Street

C.A. Gurley

1920

206 E. Middle

Caroline Peddicord

1896

203 S. Hughes

J. M. Battson

1898

107 S. Hughes (Gone)

M. F. Hale

1892

808 N . Prairie

William Evans

1905

302 S. Ardinger

A. G. Howard

1904.

85

307 West Berry
Bert Goodman
1920

409 W. Arthur
Luella Wilson
1909

411 N. Frame
Gideon Prentice
1903

511 N. Ritchie
C. C. Hartley
1913

406 N. Ardinger
Christian Church Parsonage
1921

401 E. Bird
Seth Young
1900

411 N. Ardinger
L. A. Wallace
1899

605 N. Davis
Albert Maddux
1915

302 E. Bird
A. L. Engle
1890

SWITZER-HINES HISTORIC HOME

Peter A. Switzer, Vice President of The First National Bank of Hamilton, started construction of the house at 211 East Samuel Street in 1920, and the fine brick home was completed in 1922. Mr. and Mrs. L. E. Hines bought the home in March of 1945 and it remains in the family to this day and is lovingly cared for by grandchildren and great-grandchildren.

Les Hines owned Hamilton Truck and Tractor and ran it with his son, Robert, who at the time of the home purchase was serving in an anti-aircraft division in New Guinea. Robert and his wife, Jean, were gifted the home as a wedding present in 1947 and they lived there many years. Ron and Barb Hines McDaniel grew up in the home, and their mother held kindergarten classes in the basement of the home for many years.

In January of 2024, the home was placed on the National Register of Historic Places by the National Park Service. The Register is recognized as the nation's honor roll of historic properties. The home was constructed by Brostrom & Drotts of Kansas City and the builder, C. F. McLean.

STATE OF MISSOURI
DEPARTMENT OF NATURAL RESOURCES
State Historic Preservation Office

Switzer, P . A ., Residence

Hamilton, Caldwell County, Missouri

has been officially listed in

THE NATIONAL REGISTER OF
HISTORIC PLACES

January 4, 2024
National Park Service
U.S. Department of the Interior

In recognition of the outstanding historical significance
of this property and to encourage its preservation,
we hereby affix our signatures

Michael L. Parson, Governor

Jay (Jay) Ashcroft
Secretary of State

Dru Buntin, Director
Department of Natural Resources
State Historic Preservation Officer

J. C. PENNEY HELPED ESTABLISH HAMILTON SHOE FACTORY

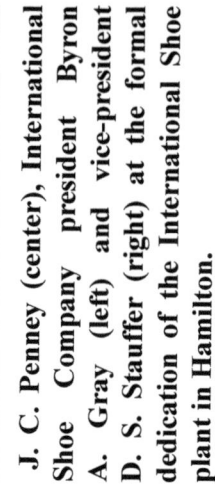

J. C. Penney (center), International Shoe Company president Byron A. Gray (left) and vice-president D. S. Stauffer (right) at the formal dedication of the International Shoe plant in Hamilton.

More than 2,000 visitors from Hamilton and surrounding communities toured the Hamilton factory of the International Shoe Company on May 15, 1948, during open house and formal dedication ceremonies at the plant.

In the early part of 1945, J. C. Penney contacted officials of the International Shoe Company about the possibility of establishing a factory in Hamilton. Soon thereafter, a representative of the company's industrial relations department came to Hamilton to meet with the Chamber of Commerce.

International Shoe proposed that Hamilton raise $45,000 to erect a 15,000 square feet building. Citizens of Hamilton, along with J. C. Penney and former Hamilton residents, would come up with $60,000 for construction of the building. The shoe company would finish off the interior of the building and also pledged to employ 200 people. The Hamilton Development Corporation (see below) would retain possession of the building with International Shoe taking a series of five-year leases.

The Hamilton Development Corporation was formed for the purpose of issuing stock in order to rasise money for purchasing the site and building the plant. L. G. Ehlers was elected president of the board of directors, with A. S. Ridley serving as vice-president; M. O. Ridings, secretary; J. P. Jones, treasurer, and L. C. Walling, B.A. Hawks and Myron Irwin also sitting on the board. At the board's first meeting in November of 1945, $7,200 was obtained from the original subscribers to the corporation previously mentioned, plus V. C. Eubank, L. E. Hines, Francis Hunt, Alden Longwell, J. L. Page, N. B. Stricklen, H. T. Till and R. L. Wood. J. C. Penney and his associates subscribed to $20,000 in stock of the Hamilton Development Corporation.

The site of the factory parking lot was also the site of the old stockyards, which back in the 1860s were north of the railroad tracks. The yards were moved during the 1870s to the south side of the tracks and McGaughy was opened up as a through street all the way to the west

end of town, prior to building the factory building.

In November of 1946, a Burlington crew put in a spur track from the siding by the H. H. Green elevator. Also, concrete piers for the factory water tower were poured. The water tank was mounted on a 100 feet tower, with a 50,000 gallon capacity.

Robert Hampton was employed by the development corporation as general superintendent of the construction site and worked closely with Charles Parrish, representative of International Shoe. The building was completed and 169 applications for employment were accepted on June 10, 1947. Production at the plant soon began and quickly reached a level of 3,000 pairs of baby shoes daily through the work of 225 employees.

International Shoe Company closed its Hamilton plant in June of 1965, citing a reduced demand by the public for the type of shoe manufactured at the plant.

After several unsuccessful tries at locating a manufacturing plant of some kind in the building, the Hamilton Development Corporation succeeded in reaching an agreement with Weber Shoe Company of Tipton, MO, a subsidiary of Green Shoe Manufacturing Company, manufacturers of Stride-Rite shoes, to locate a plant in Hamilton in August of 1965. Bill Branam was hired as local factory superintendent,

Rosamond Sturgis went to work in the office, and Emma Tomlin was fitting room floor lady. All three were still with the company in 1990. Stride-Rite Company purchased the building from the Hamilton Development Corporation in September of 1985 and became the largest employer in Hamilton and Caldwell County with some 300 workers manufacturing quality baby shoes.

However, the factory closed in 1997 when operations were shipped to Mexico and South America. Midwest Gloves, based in Chillicothe, bought the property and operated out of the facility for a time. Missouri Star Quilt Company currently owns and utilizes the building.

89

International Shoe. A formal dedication ceremony was held for International Shoe in May of 1948. D. R. Gillilan was the first superintendent, and other positions were held by Tom Christman, office manager; June Thomson, personnel officer; Harry Goff, plant engineer; Marvin Beller, lasting room foreman; Bea S. Widerman, fitting room foreman; Paul G. Sherman, cutting room foreman; Edgar P. Hafner, packing room foreman, and Fred F. Ochs, bottoming room foreman. Familiar faces on the front row of this photos of the 1948 work force include Darlene McIntosh, Veta Holman, Dorothy Linville, Ann Milligan, Belle Bacon, Ruth Galpin and Wanda Smittle. You can probably pick out many others.

The Stride-Rite Company, (left) 1990.

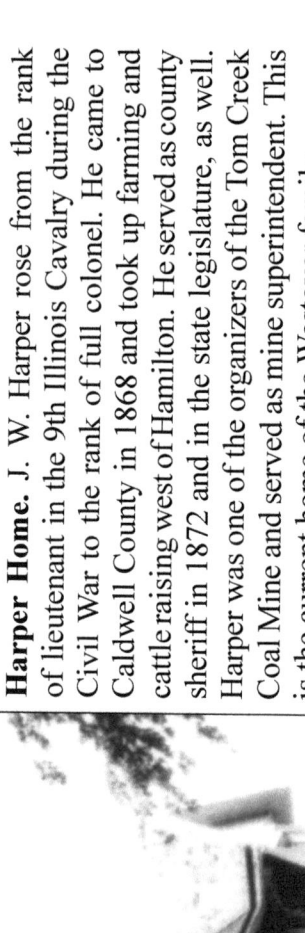

Dr. J. M. Donaldson Home. Dr. J. M. Donaldson was a native Missourian and graduate of St. Louis Medical College in 1872 before coming to Hamilton.

Harper Home. J. W. Harper rose from the rank of lieutenant in the 9th Illinois Cavalry during the Civil War to the rank of full colonel. He came to Caldwell County in 1868 and took up farming and cattle raising west of Hamilton. He served as county sheriff in 1872 and in the state legislature, as well. Harper was one of the organizers of the Tom Creek Coal Mine and served as mine superintendent. This is the current home of the Westover family.

Amber's Department Store. Mrs. Harold L. "Amber" Bowen was a daughter of Frank L. Royer, who operated a cigar factory (maker of the famous "113" cigar) over the First National Bank. Amber was a bookkeeper for Parrish Hardware for 13 years. She graduated from LaDue College of Beauty Culture in 1929 and opened a beauty shop in 1930. She bought the Fowlery Ready to Wear Millinery in 1932 and in 1939 moved to the McClean building to obtain more floor and window display space. She bought the hotel building and twin-room store building in 1940.

McLean The Clothier. J. W. McLean operated one of the finest, most up-to-date men's clothing stores in the area for more than 30 years, beginning just after the turn of the 20th Century. "Always Early With the Latest" was the theme of the day for McLeans, which operated first in the building later occupied by Strade Photography (now the Sewing Center) and then later in the Richmond building adjacent to the Hamilton Hotel.

Hales Market. This photo taken in front of Hales Market in January of 1953 illustrates the new metal street signs that replaced old, obsolete wooden markers. The Hamilton Community Gardeners Club sponsored the movement to modernize Hamilton's street markers.

Bennett Grocery. William Bennett bought the Pederson grocery business on North Davis in March of 1927 but had previously been in business six years at another site. The building is gone.

Highland Cemetery North Gates. Fred Thwing, a Hamilton native but later a Kansas City real estate investor, erected an iron fence and gate monuments at the north entrance to Highland Cemetery in memory of his parents, Charles and Harriett Thwing, in November of 1925. Both are buried in Highland.

93

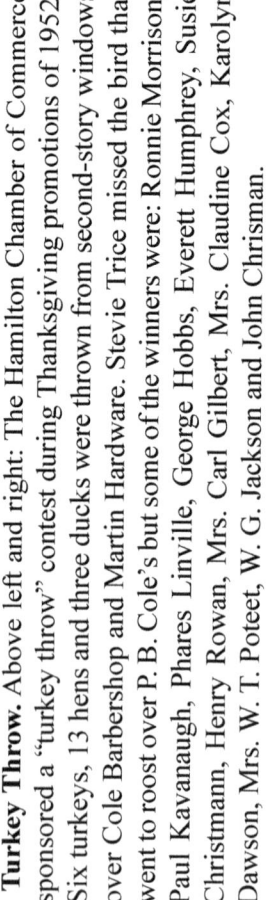

Turkey Throw. Above left and right: The Hamilton Chamber of Commerce sponsored a "turkey throw" contest during Thanksgiving promotions of 1952. Six turkeys, 13 hens and three ducks were thrown from second-story windows over Cole Barbershop and Martin Hardware. Stevie Trice missed the bird that went to roost over P. B. Cole's but some of the winners were: Ronnie Morrison, Paul Kavanaugh, Phares Linville, George Hobbs, Everett Humphrey, Susie Christmann, Henry Rowan, Mrs. Carl Gilbert, Mrs. Claudine Cox, Karolyn Dawson, Mrs. W. T. Poteet, W. G. Jackson and John Chrisman.

Liberty Bell. Right–The Liberty Bell stopped in Hamilton in May of 1950 and was exhibited to pupils at the south side grade school. The three girls standing on the truck are Donna Matchett (in rear), Bonnie Kay Barnes and Margaret Sue Thomson. The boys examining the inside of the bell are Donald Wayne Walker and Robert Creekmore. The bell, weighing 2,080 pounds, was one of 52 replicas that toured the country during the 1950 Independence Savings Bond Drive.

Turn of the century Davis Street. This photo shows a number of interesting sights no longer seen—the Burlington Hotel above the Sewing Center building, the balcony over the Hamilton Hotel (first building on the left), the public windmill north of today's Hy-Klas building and the magnificent Tiffin building in the distance to the north. (Photo courtesy of Johnnie Henderson.

Old Broadway. This turn-of-the-century photo shows Hamilton's first main thoroughfare, Ardinger Street, or Broadway as it was known then. On the left is the Moore Monument business north of Dr. Tinsley Brown's home. The Wallace produce business was in the building now Ed Ernat's machine shop. You can see the spire atop the old Presbyterian Church farther up the street.

207 E. School
C. H. Lampton
1915

607 N. Davis
Frank Parrish
1894

J. F. Colby (gone)
1870s

400 N. Ewing
Alston Bowman
1893

601 N. Ardinger
George Richardson
Before 1915

210 S. Ardinger
Robert D. Paxton
1880s

401 E. Arthur
Taylor Allee
1894

503 W. Berry
John Bauer
1907

302 N. Gallatin
M. E. Overstreet
1939

96

701 N. Davis
D. P. Martin
1881

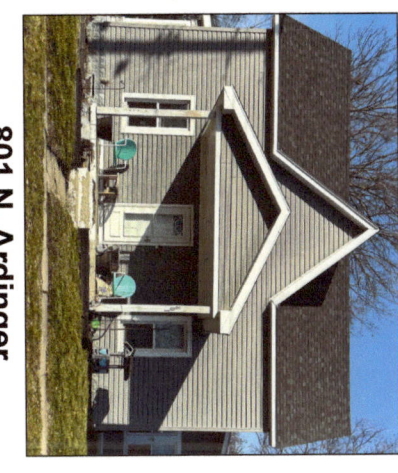

801 N. Ardinger
Elva Dennison
1895

310 E. Bird
Maud Harlow
1920

201 E. Bird
Anthony Rohrbough
1870

210 E. Arthur
E. H. Daley
1891

301 N. Ardinger
Bud Hawks
1941

611 W. McGaughy
George Snyder
1890

311 N. Hughes
Otis Richardson
1860

201 E. School
A. R. McAdoo
1890s–Gone

1919 HHS Senior Class: Back row, left to right: Helen Boutwell, Stanley Douglas, Owen Kinne, David Turner, Dotty Lyon, Roselle Ganser, Ruth McCubbin and Mary Alexander. Front row, left to right: Lavella Carr, Maurine Rauber, Maurine Hooker, Irene Kemper, Grace Burnett, Alice Kennedy, Fern Gibson, Carmen Cook, Mildred Anderson and Beulah Snyder.

98

HAMILTON MEDICAL CENTERS

Hamilton Medical Center and Pharmacy. With the retirement of Dr. Frank Daley, local citizens were concerned about being without primary health care. A volunteer board of directors was formed to explore the option of applying for an FQHC grant/Federally Qualified Health Center to recruit physicians and build a clinic to serve our communities.

A clinic was built on Cross Street to offer primary health and optometry care, opening in 1983. Providers at the clinic were new medical graduates who were serving for the opportunity to receive forgiveness of a portion of their medical school debt.

CCMAC in later years merged with Northwest Health Services from Mound City. Primary health care expanded to include pharmacy, dental and mental health services.

Hamilton Family Health Center. A satellite clinic for Cameron Regional Medical Center, the Hamilton Family Health Center delivers primary care in an outpatient setting. The clinic's first location in Hamilton in 1993 was in the center block of Davis Street, east side. The new facility, built in 2013, is at the corner of Davis and Berry streets.

FUTURE FARMERS OF AMERICA 1955-56

Front row, from left: Marvin Nickell (advisor), Jim Cox, Larry Henry, Robert Cox, Jim Black, Lynn Arms, Bill Henley and J. W. Linville.
Row two: Kent Adkison, Ronnie McGlothlin, Sam Milligan, Danny Connor, Bill Guffey, Harlan Buck, Pharis Linville, Ralph Summers, Larry Logston, Tony McGlothlin and Randy Berry.
Row three: Everett Humphrey, Larry Bowers, Barry Alexander, Ron Corbett, Gerald Arms, Gerald Wilson, Clifford (Bud) Sloan, Dean Adkison and Phil Wood.
Row four: Dale Hartley, Barry Cornelius, Bill Vance, Gene Martin, Jack Riley, John Gaume, Gary Stone ad Gale Linville.
Row five: Norman Edwards, Donnie Bowman, Jerry Bebout, Joe Potts, Clarence Innis, Roger Summers, Garland Rice and Bob Blann.

Hamilton Grandstands

HAMILTON GRANDSTAND

No. Mo. State Fair — Sept. 2, 1919 to Sept. 10, 1930
American Legion Race Meets — July 27, 1932 to Aug. 1950
No. Mo. Steam and Gas Engine Shows Aug. 22, 1964 to Aug. 1985
Hamilton School sports till 1985 (Burned Jan. 19, 1987)

A fire of underdetermined origin in the early morning hours of Jan. 19, 1987, destroyed the 80-year-old wooden grandstand at the Penney High School football field. The fire occurred just two days before the structure was slated for demolition. The building was wired for electricity and an insurance adjustor found no signs of arson. The fire was discovered by Frank Helm, night watchman at the Stride-Rite Shoe Co.

The old grandstand had been declared unsafe and was unavailable for Hamilton's first ever football playoff game in November of 1986. The new grandstand, built soon after, has withstood the test of time.

The Tiffin Building

W. J. McBrayer Home

As They Were.....

Dr. W. T. Lindley Home

Dr. Will Aplin Home

Will Aplin Home

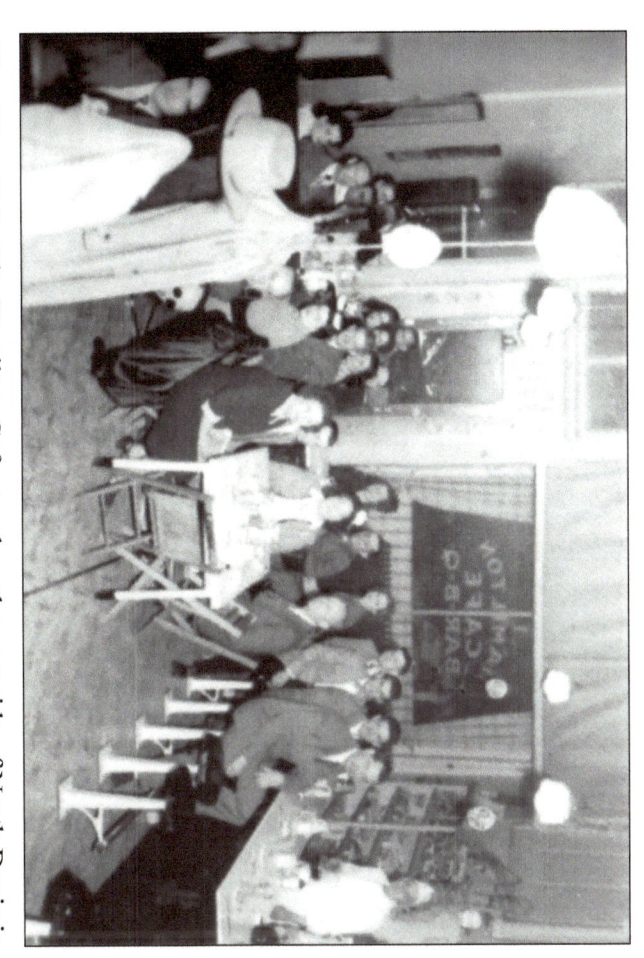

Hamilton Cafe. The Hamilton Cafe stood on the east side of North Davis in the block of buildings that burned in the 1966 fire.

Whitey Herzog. Former Kansas City Royals and St. Louis Cardinals baseball manager Whitey Herzog was visiting in town in 1979 with Conner and Norma Jones at the Hamilton Locker. Herzog was a great friend of Dale and Nelle Scott.

Coffee Gang. Left–Hamiltonians have always loved gathering at a local cafe to discuss current events. This photo, taken during the 1960s at Eben's Cafe, includes Ira Elliott, Ed Strade, Sherman Henkins, M. E. Thomson, P. A. Oldfield, Lewis Gregory, Mrs. Sam (Muriel) Evans, Jim White, Robert Grant, L. G. Ehlers, Connor Jones, Bob Hines, Jim Moore, Roy Morris, Oscar Axon, John Wynne, Fletcher Gammill, Charley Gregory, Roy Huey and Eben Jones.

Anderson Home. Joseph Anderson owned part interest in the Anderson Brothers Dry Goods Emporium, with his brother Wallace, during the latter part of the 19th Century and early 1900s. Joseph built the home after the frame familly house on the same site burned. The Henry Conrad family lived there and Owen Adams operated a flower shop out of the home, before selling it to the Wayne Oberhelmans, who later sold it to the Westover family.

McAdoo Home. Lawrence McAdoo was born in Hamilton, the son of A. R. McAdoo. He was engineer at the Caldwell Coal Mine east of town for several years before going into the grocery business and operating the Hamilton Canning Factory. This is the home of Roger and Julie Hill.

Hamburger Inn. Mr. and Mrs. Leslie Decker of Cameron purchased the hamburger stand on West Berry in November of 1927 and named it The Hamburger Inn.

Irwin Motor Company. Myron Irwin started Irwin Motor Company in 1932, selling Dodge and Plymouth automobiles. He took over the two-story frame building on today's site of Missouri Star Quilt Company main shop, in 1937 when he switched to a Nash dealership. This photo was taken in 1949 just before the building was torn down. Irwin built the present building as a showroom with second floor apartments and a garage to the rear.

The Hamburger Inn

Open Saturday, Nov. 19

Have remodeled the lunch stand next to Standard Oil Filling Station on Mill Street.

Come In and Get a Free Cup

of Coffee Saturday with your purchases

Pie	10c	Hamburger Sand-
		wiches 5c
Coffee	5c	Chili 10c

Leslie Decker, Prop.

"Quick Courteous Service"

Pride of St. Louis at the Till Theatre. The biographical film on the life of Jerome "Dizzy" Dean premiered at the Till Theatre in 1952. Released by 20th Century Fox, it detailed Dean's rise to stardom with the St. Louis Baseball Cardinals.

106

Off to War: Young men from Caldwell County posed for the camera as they got ready to go off to fight in World War I.

507 N. Burruss
John Cowley
1907

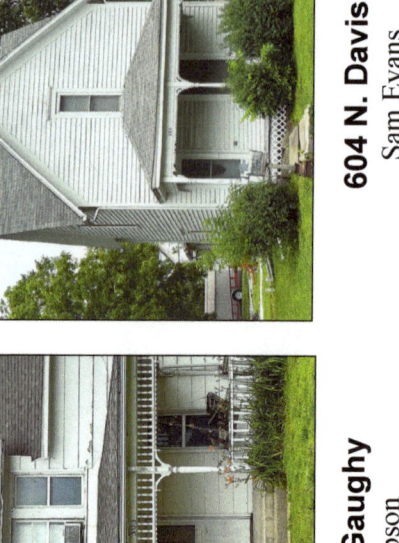

604 N. Davis
Sam Evans
1885

203 E. Arthur
F. E. Whitman
1920

303 E. McGaughy
Fred Gibson
1880s

201 W. Samuel
John Morton
1886-Gone

609 N. Burruss
Lawrence McAdoo
1908

711 N. Ardinger
L. D. Van Valkenburg
1880s

410 N. Ardinger
James Giddings
1898

213 N. California
Irene Austin
1890s

108

410 N. Burruss
True D. Parr
1920

310 N. Burruss
John Stagner
1892

109 S. Hughes
Dr. Neill Johnson
1918

208 E. Arthur
Emma & Sarah Chain
1907

510 E. Bird
W. W. Crockett
1905-Gone

201 E. Samuel
Frank Bowman
1921

611 N. Ardinger
Thomas Gibson
1895

NW Putnam Rd.
E. B. Vaughn
1912

501 E. Arthur
Donald Martin
1921

300 N. Prairie
A. W. Daley
1899

400 E. Arthur
George McPherson
Before 1915

301 E. 6th
John Sweem
1923

511 N. Ardinger
George Dunlap
1924

409 E. 6th
G. W. Adams
1897

203 N. Gallatin
L. G. Ehlers
1939

408 E. Arthur
J. E. Lenhart
Before 1898

501 N. Burruss
C. P. Hudson
1916

404 E. Arthur
John Watkinson
1904

110

AUGUST 21, 2017
SOLAR ECLIPSE

Vicki (Mogg) Ward took this photo of the summer of 2017 total solar eclipse. The shot was taken on Davis Street looking south from in front of HyKlas Food and Family Center. Dubbed as the "Great American Solar Eclipse" by the media, it was visible within a band that spanned the contiguous United States, from the Pacific to the Atlantic coasts.

Despite the overcast clouds, street lights came on in the middle of the afternoon, and birds and animals began exhibiting night time behavior due to the passing of the moon in front of the sun.

The 2017 eclipse was the first solar eclipse visible across the entirety of the US since June 8, 1918. Not since the February 1979 eclipse had a total eclipse been visible from anywhere in the mainland United States. The next solar eclipse occurred on April 8, 2024.

Hamilton Hotel Demolition

Attempts to save the old Hamilton Hotel building, erected after the 1883 fire, failed and it was demolished in the summer of 1993, along with the Richmond Department Store building on the north end. The C. B. Franke stone atop the hotel has been preserved and rededicated.

Franke Block History

Charles B. Franke was a perfect example of an enterprising American of the 19th Century. Born in New York in 1841, Franke received what was then considered a classical education.

At the age of 18, Franke enlisted in a New York infantry regiment famous for flashy uniforms patterned after the French who fought in North Africa. Franke served two terms of enlistment in the Army of the Potomac and was present at some of the Civil War's bloodiest battles, including Antietam, Gettysburg and The Wilderness. He was present at Appomattox in 1865 when Robert E. Lee surrendered the Army of Northern Virginia to Ulysses S. Grant. Franke mustered out in October of 1865 at Governor's Island, NY.

Franke soon entered public life in the employ of the U. S. Treasury Department in Washington, DC and was a frequent traveler. He perhaps passed through Hamilton during his travels and a favorable impression may have led to him settling here in 1878.

Upon arrival in Hamilton, Franke operated a dry goods business in the middle of the center block on the east side.

A disaster in 1883 opened the door to greater opportunities for Franke. After a fire destroyed most of the west-center block of wooden frame buildings, notably housing the Western Hotel, Franke bought all four vacant lots, now occupied by the Penney Park, and built a brick hotel on lots 1 and 2, and a double room retail space on lots 3 and 4. Subsequent names of the hotel were Franke Hotel, Rhodes House, Hotel dePorter and lastly Hamilton Hotel. The basement of the hotel once housed a barber shop across the street from the train depot.

The north rooms at first housed a billiard hall run by Franke and his brother, and a mercantile business, also operated by the two brothers. Over the years this double building has been occupied by a shoe store, saloon, pool room, lyric theatre and three notable merchandise stores: McLeans Clothier, Amber's Department Store and lastly the Richmond Department Store, run by J. R. and Lou Ann Richmond.

Franke would sell his buildings and business interests to brothers John and Mont Hale in 1886. The Hales would eventually move their mercantile business to the opposite end of the block and would hire a young farm boy, James Cash Penney, to work in the store. Soon after, Franke took ownership of the 3-story Harry House, an old hotel located at the corner of Berry and Ardinger Streets where the original MSQ store is located. This hotel, built in 1869, would compete with several others for customers traveling by train. However, it wasn't long before the Franke name disappeared from Hamilton history.

After first trying to save the failing hotel building under private ownership, it was torn down during the summer of 1993, ending 109 years of history on this site, but today the Franke's Block history, in a sense, has come full circle. The capstone, once centered at the roof level between the hotel and retail buildings, facing Davis Street, survived the demolition and has been repaired and mounted on a cement base, with a plaque briefly detailing its history. Passersby may now pause and read that history in the same spot where the capstone once greeted passersby on Hamilton's main thoroughfare.

Temple Hotel. This home, built in 1912, was for many years a hotel/boarding house. E. L. Temple operated a hotel here, beginning in the 1920s, but sold the hotel to L. L. Bentley in 1932.

Mrs. Bentley would serve 50-cent chicken dinners to lodgers on Sunday. Subsequent owners included Orron Surface, and E. E. Alexander. The business was leased many times under every ownership. It was a popular boarding spot for teachers at the nearby high school.

Country home. The old Clough house stood just south of town off of Highway 13 but was torn down in February of 1950 to make way for the home of R. C. McNary. The 28-room house had four chimneys and three fireplaces. Studding throughout the entire house was done with 2x6 material. The Clough farm was known as the Highland Stock Farm around 1915.

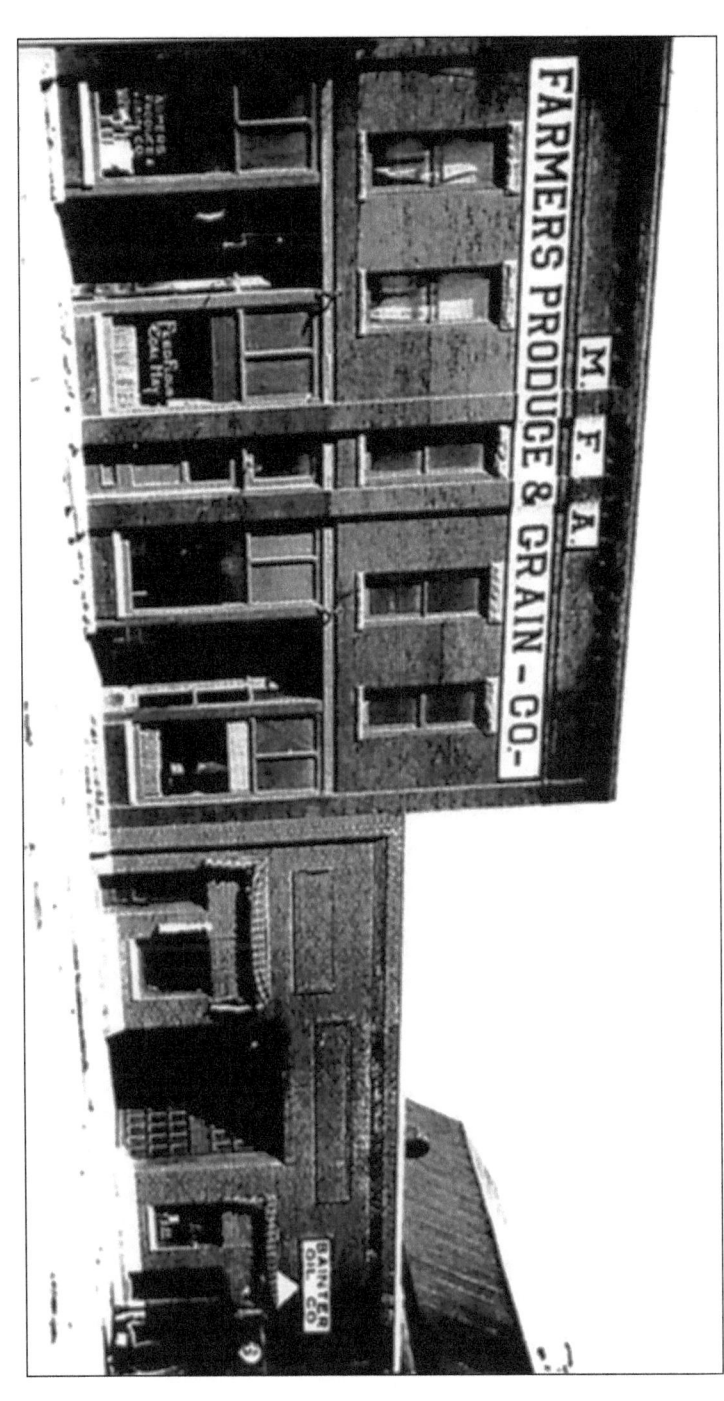

HAMILTON LOCKER
Box 117
HAMILTON, MISSOURI 64644

LOCKER RENTAL
WHOLESALE · RETAIL
FREEZER MEATS
SLAUGHTERING

CONNOR (PETE) JONES
OWNER · MANAGER

Bus. Ph.: 816-583-2126
HOME Ph.: 816-583-4422

Farmers Produce & Grain. The MFA Exchange was incorporated in Hamilton on April 5, 1920, with 228 farmers listed in the articles. The Farmers Produce & Grain Co. occupied the Hamilton Locker building when this picture was taken. "Mood" Aldridge ran a barbershop in the south end of the Bainter Oil Co. building. The Dannen elevator can be seen to the north.

Hamilton Locker. The Hamilton Locker crew from the 1960s: from left to right are Zona "Skip" Dunn, George Dodge, Norma and Connor Jones, Leo Lynch and Fletcher Gammill.

An offshoot of the Farmers Produce & Grain Company, the Hamilton Farmer Locker System, managed by R. J. Potter, opened on June 13, 1942. The frozen food locker system was considered a modern method of refrigerated food preservation, with 300 individual lockers available for use by the public.

Blue Castle Cafe. The Blue Castle opened in 1920 on Old Highway 36, just west of the stoplight. The house specialty was a brain sandwich. Some, but not all owner/operators were: J. M. Kizer, Alex Warden, James Edwards, Bill Kuhnert, Orville Gooding, Lehman Page, Russell Bretz and Ira Elliott. The cafe closed in the 1970s, but part of the old building remains.

1940 HHS Football Team. This unorthodox shot of the 1940 Hamilton High School football starting eleven was taken between the train depot and the public library building.

North Missouri Steam and Gas Engine Show

One of the largest crowds in years thronged to Hamilton on Aug. 22 and 23, 1964, to attend the first annual North Missouri Steam and Gas Engine Antique Show and Demonstration. This was a new event for the area and drew exhibitors from a wide area and a large crowd of spectators from as far away as Illinois, Iowa and Kansas.

Drexel Hill and Jack Neal were chosen co-chairmen of the Steam and Gas Engine Association, and Ryland Miller and Jim Henry served as co-secretaries. Also among the show's founders were Russell Moss, Clarence McCutchan, Paul Bryant, Lynn Hamlet, Dale Oldfield, Reuben Hartley, Virgil Rains, Blake Corbett, Casey Rhinehart, Nelson Rhinehart, Clarence Drumm, Bob Baker, Dale Hartley, Bob Michael, Sherman Henkins, Ralph McNary, M. U. McCrary, J. R. Richmond, Ben Woody, Irvin Esry, Charles Rouse, Dean Trosper, Earl Miller, Lee Roy Huey, Carl Ford, Roy Hendren, Archie Nibarger, Ralph Blades and E. C. Kavanaugh.

Tom Neil and Burns Corbett furnished the horse teams that cut the first oats on the Harley Ayers farm, and Russell Moss supplied the binder. Moss and Clarence McCutchan were in charge of old equipment displays at the very first show.

Over time, especially with establishment of a new softball/baseball complex at Penney High School, and eventually a new elementary school, the show outgrew the grounds behind and to the north of the football stadium. The Association purchased 20 acres of land west of Hamilton, off State Road CC, in 2007 and the first show was held there the following year. The show celebrated its 60th year in 2023.

Working in the wheat. (Above, right) Elaine Moss Curtis, president of the 1980 North Missouri Steam and Gas Engine Show, works the binder during wheat cutting for the 1980 show. Clarence McCutchan, one of the original organizers of the annual event, gives her a helping hand.
Russell Moss. Russell Moss, (right) another Steam and Gas Engine Show organizer in 1964, was one of the men most responsible for making the show one of the biggest and best of its kind today in the Midwest.

118

HISTORICAL BUILDINGS

First Martin Building. The present Olive & Honey building on North Davis was erected by F. A. Martin in 1898 after Martin purchased the George Rogers Drug Store. Martin kept the building until his death in 1924, when his son, Donald, took over the business. Donald Martin sold the business to Sam McMaster and upon McMaster's passing, Guy Thomson bought the business and it operated for many years as Thomson Hardware. Irston Alden ran a hardware store here in the 1980s and 90s. It was later Tammy's Flowers.

Second Martin Building. F. A. Martin bought the old Phoenix Hotel in 1900 and tore down the wooden frame building, which was erected in 1868-69 by E. C. Kelso. Asa Thomson operated the hotel for a time. The third story of the old hotel building was a meeting place for the Odd Fellows lodge. Asa Thomson's son, Guy, helped tear down the old building and helped construct the present building. Martin erected the building in 1902 and would soon sell to the Missouri Dry Goods Company. The building was divided into two rooms when C. J. Gurley acquired it in 1940 and moved the Monarch Hatchery into the north room, while he rented out the south room for a skating rink.

Many will remember this site as Gamble's, run by Ross Hicklin, and later the Ole Granary Restaurant, operated by the Thornton family.

At this writing in the summer of 2024, the building's future is in jeopardy due to structural problems.

HISTORY OF THE HAMILTON PUBLIC LIBRARY

"I am making an effort to start a circulating library, and I respectfully ask support and assistance from the good people of Hamilton and vicinity. I propose to get 100 standard and readable books. No cheap books. I will charge $1 for the use of the library for six months. You all recognize the need of such an institution. Help me make it a success."

Those words from Clarence A. Green appeared in an advertisement in *The Hamiltonian* in November of 1880 and sparked an instant response from the people of Hamilton, who threw their support to what they recognized as a worthwhile project. On January 14, 1881, Mr. Green advertised that the library was now set up and ready for use. Green, a scholar having educated himself for the ministry, died in March of 1881.

Charles H. Boroff then conducted a circulating library at the post office book store for several years, presumably taking over the one started by Green. In 1885, the members of the circulating library and the Hamilton Reading Circle organized a Hamilton Library Assocation. The first officers were H. H. Rogers, president; A. R. Torrey, secretary, and J. N. Morton, treasurer. They were assisted by the Women's Christian Temperance Union (WCTU) librarians. The association bought 100 books and they were placed in the WCTU reading room. In August of 1886, the ladies resigned as managers and the books were moved to the office of H. W. Markham, real estate agent, and later to a library room set up in Morton's hardware building.

In 1897, Superintendent J. C. Pike of the Hamilton School reported the high school as having a library of approximately 250 books, some being from the old Hamilton Library Association. The high school library was open to the public from 2 p.m. until 5 p.m. on Wednesdays and Saturdays and was presided over by Mrs. W. C. (Alice Aplin) McCoy, who worked at a wage of $1 per week–half paid by the city and half paid by the school. Mrs. McCoy served faithfully as librarian of the circulating department of the high school library for 18 years.

In November of 1919, nearly half of the 3,000 books that were then housed in the school library were destroyed when the north side high school burned. Books that were salvaged from the fire were housed in a building located on Davis Street, where librarian service continued under Mrs. McCoy for a time, and later under Miss Mabel White.

Home Culture Club promotes library

In 1918 and 1919, ladies of the Home Culture Club promoted the idea of a permanent public library building for Hamilton. On March 7, 1919, club members petitioned the Hamilton City Council for a one mill tax for library support to provide a permanent maintenance fund for the library. Acting on their petition, aldermen presented the tax measure to residents in the April election and won voter approval from the citizens of Hamilton by a vote of 109 for and 45 against. This tax would raise about $700 annually for the support of the library.

First public library board

Following passage of the library tax, the Hamilton Public Library Board was formed with Elmer E. Clark, president; Mrs. J. W. McLean, vice-president, and Miss Maud Dawson, secretary. Other board members were Mrs. True D. Parr, F. L. Bowman, James E. Goldsberry and Harvey L. Bainter. Mrs. Parr served less than a year before resigning due to poor health and Miss Katherine Houghton took her place on the board.

In the meantime, members of the Home Culture Club were still supportive of the idea of a permanent home for the library. Some of the club leaders wrote to native son and former Hamilton resident, J. C. Penney, about the matter and Penney consented to donate $10,000 for building a library, conditional on the people of Hamilton and vicinity contributing a minimum of $5,000 to be used in purchasing a site and equipping the building.

Through efforts of the Hamilton Library Board, the money was raised. E. E. Clark and other board members worked tirelessly in circulating petitions asking for subscriptions to the building fund and these efforts resulted in 413 subscribers and raised $18,661.82. Of this amount, J. C. Penney gave $10,000 as a memorial to his parents, and other family members gave $1,200. The Home Culture Club, P.E.O. Sisterhood,

D.A.R. Chapter and a number of other individuals made substantial contributions of equipment and books.

In January of 1920, the library board purchased one lot and part of another south of the Chicago, Burlington & Quincy Railroad park on Broadway from L. L. Grigsby for the sum of $1,250. Mr. Grigsby also gave a personal gift to the library board of a triangular piece of land adjoining the site.

Robert E. Peden of Kansas City, MO was selected as architect for the new building in February, and in August of 1920 sealed bids for construction were accepted. Mosby & Goodrich, contractors from Kansas City, received the job with a bid of $15,700. Work on the building began on Aug. 24, 1920.

Miss Mabel White was selected to serve as the Hamilton Public Library's first librarian at a salary of $10 per week. The new library opened to the public on Feb. 12, 1921, with no formal dedication.

Later librarians

Mrs. Lois McFadden served the library capably for 37 years, beginning in March of 1922. Under her leadership, all the books were catalogued in accordance with the Dewey Decimal System. Mrs. McFadden served as librarian until September of 1959, when ill health forced her to resign.

Mrs. Hazel Bellante followed as librarian for one year and was succeeded by Mrs. Guy King, who served ten years before resigning in January of 1970. Mrs. Birch (Helen) Mackey was immediately hired by the library board to fill the position of librarian.

From 1972-1976, an agreement between the library board and Hamilton R-II Schools allowed the school to rent the Hamilton Public Library basement to use as a classroom for morning and afternoon kindergarten classes. Through the years, county and city elections were also often held in the library basement. *(The above information was contributed by longtime librarian, Delores Humphrey.)*

Library finds new home

A group of Hamilton citizens met on May 2, 1974, to discuss the possibility of a new home for the Hamilton Public Library. Plans were initiated to build a combined library-museum building to be named in memory of J. C. Penney, who died in 1971. Construction plans called for a 40 x 100 foot, one-level brick structure containing two wings-one housing the new library and the other housing J. C. Penney memorabilia. The lower level of the building would include a community room with a large kitchen.

Old Hamilton Public Library. Erected in 1920, the old library served for years as a meeting hall for the Masonic Lodge, before being sold to Missouri Star Quilt Company.

Dean Hales and M. O. Ridings became co-chairmen of the J. C. Penney Memorial Library and Museum fund-raising committee. E. R. (Bob) Penney, a nephew of J. C. Penney, assisted with the project and was instrumental in helping raise the necessary funds. Family members, friends and former associates of J. C. Penney, as well as many local people, contributed to the project. The Penney family, J. C. Penney Company, Inc. and the J. C. Penney Foundation each contributed $25,000. Friends and residents of Hamilton also contributed $25,000.

Dean Faulkender, architect, was employed in June of 1975 when the building site was prepared. The general contract for construction was awarded to Richardson Construction Company of Hamilton and excavation began in September.

Mrs. Mackey, library board members and other individuals moved the contents of the old library into the room provided for the Hamilton Public Library in the new J. C. Penney Memorial Library and Museum building. For business reasons it was decided to retain the original name of the Hamilton Public Library.

The new building was formally dedicated on April 11, 1976. Bob Penney served as master of ceremonies and Mrs. J. C. Penney was among the honored guests.

Mrs. Mackey submitted her resignation to the library board in May of 1976 and Miss Delores Humphrey was selected to fill her vacancy. On Aug. 3, 1976, citizens approved a levy increase, bringing the total library tax to 2-1/2 mills or 25 cents on the $100 of assessed valuation. With increased revenue, money was once more available for much needed books, magazines and library supplies. Another tax issue passed in April of 1989 when the library faced another fiscal crisis.

Thanks to the tax support, Hamilton residents receive a library card free of charge. Two local organizations, the Home Culture Club and the Literary Study Club, were consistent supporters of the library, contributing money each year to support operations, just as the original members of Home Culture Club did in the early years of the institution.

Library since 2022

Current Head Librarian Sonja Farnsworth took the reins in August of 2022. Along with her staff, the library officially added STEAM (Science-Technology-Art-Math) kits, both for use in the library and in circulation. The STEAM program is to make learning these topics fun. The library has robots and games that also add to the learning experience. An in-person story hour was also restarted.

Summer reading program donations have doubled, as well as more community involvement in the form of guest readers for story time, and an increase in donations of books as well as money. The library has sponsored three Story Walks. Many improvements and new programs have been made possible through grants.

The Hamilton Library was recognized by The State Library and National Museum and Libraries for the STEAM grants program and its execution.

Current library board members in 2024 were Candy Hensley, president; Susan Pipkin, vice president; Misty Doan, secretary; Sarah Connelly, treasurer; Sydney Ernat, Julie Dawson, Liz Gutinatus, Sarah Crawford. Immediate past board members were Liz Little, Nicole Montero and Renae Anderson.

Vaughn Grocery. J. W. Vaughn bought the Bennett grocery business in April of 1930 in the middle of the north block of Davis Street, west side. The Vaughns operated the store into the 1940s. During the 1930s there were seven grocery stores in Hamilton: Vaughn, Johnson, Haney, Places, Glick, and Hawkins, O. C. Howard and A & P Food Store. Leo Hales purchased the Johnson grocery store in January of 1938.

123

Main street scene. Cook Photographers captured a northbound car in motion in this early 1950s street scene of North Davis. Notice the train in motion in the background.

Junction Cafe. This site was first occupied in 1882 by Gideon Preentice, who built a two-story brick building (later destroyed in the 1886 fire) for his hardware bsiness. Other occupants have been the Boston Racket Store, Missouri Power & Light and the Lyric Movie Theatre (upstairs). The Junction Cafe was the ticket office for the Santa Fe Trailways bus line starting under the management of Walter Wheeler. Irston and Lucille Alden ran the Colonial Cafe in the location in the 1960s and 70s.

Women of Substance

Kidder Institute Graduates

Dr. Bertha Booth. Women have always played a prominent role in Hamilton's progress and growth. Dr. Bertha Booth nearly single-handily kept Hamilton's early history alive through her tireless research and in-person interviews of early settlers. An 1893 Hamilton High School graduate (and classmate of J. C. Penney), Dr. Booth received her second level of education at Kidder Institute. Dr. Booth went on to earn a PhD. in history and languages from the University of Chicago, and she later taught in several small colleges and major universities, including the University of Missouri and University of Arkansas.

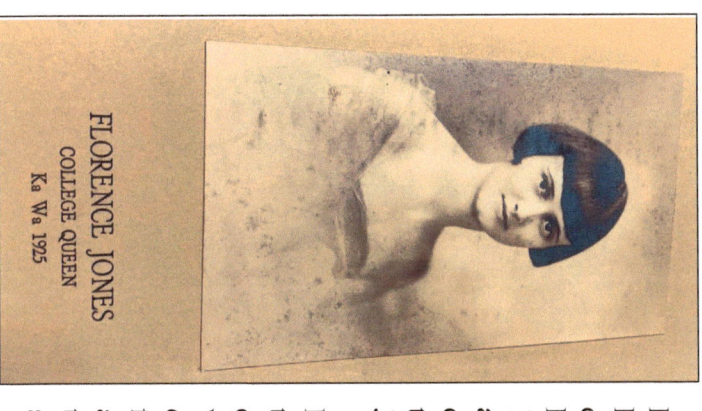

FLORENCE JONES
COLLEGE QUEEN
Ka Wa 1925

Florence Jones. A beloved teacher at HHS, Penney High School and Shaw Memorial Junior High School, Florence Jones also received an education from Kidder institute. A native of Dawn, Missouri, Miss Jones was the college queen in 1925 and her photo appeared on this cover of the Ka-Wa, the annual of Kidder Junior College.

Upon graduation, Miss Jones taught in the Pleasant Ridge country school. She was a well-liked disciplinarian, and finished her teaching after many years in the Hamilton School system.

Miss Florence Jones
Science and Cont. Issues

Dr. Bertha Booth was one of Hamilton's first historians.

The cast of "The Gypsy Troubadour," presented by Hamilton High School students of 1943.

W. J. Clark home. The Wilbur Clark home in the east end of town, later occupied by his son, Frank E. Clark, was torn down in the late 1970s. Jim Mogg owns the lot where the house once stood. (Photo courtesy of Bob Grant, Jr.)

Ayr-Vu Motel (left). Mr. and Mrs. Herbert Connor operated a hotel out of their home during the 1940s. Before that, Dr. Lyle Daley ran a hospital out of the house where he lived for a time. The house was built in 1880 by Frank Clark for his new bride.

Edward Kennedy Home. The Standard Oil Company bought the Ed Kennedy home at the corner of Davis and Berry streets in 1926 in order to erect a service station on the site. The house was moved south on the lots retained by the Kennedys.

The Hamilton High School band of 1937 won many awards, including first place in the national contest held in Lawrence, KS. The Hamilton band also represented Missouri in contests in Des Moines (1936) and Omaha (1938).

Hamilton City Park. Right: This wintertime photo shows the old geezbo at the city park. The view is looking south and the large house of the late Leonard Orr can be seen in the background. The old city park was the site of many Chautauqua celebrations and other special occasions, such as picnics, tent revivals, concerts and Fourth of July celebrations that featured brass bands, orchestras and patriotic readings.

The Clark-Craven-Boutwell-Eads Post of the American Legion sponsored a memorial service in the park on August 10, 1923, asking citizens to pause for one hour in observance of the funeral of President Warren G. Harding in Marion, Ohio.

With many activities shifting to the American Legion grounds north of town, the park was turned into a ballfield in the 1950s. It remains a site for youth sports activities.

Hamilton's water plant. Lower left: This photo shows the Hamilton Municipal Waterworks as it looked during the late 1940s

129

Water Plant employees. Lower right: Bill Kuhnert and water superintendent John Sweem in front of the water plant in 1949. Kuhnert later served as superintendent.,

Hamilton Telephone Company

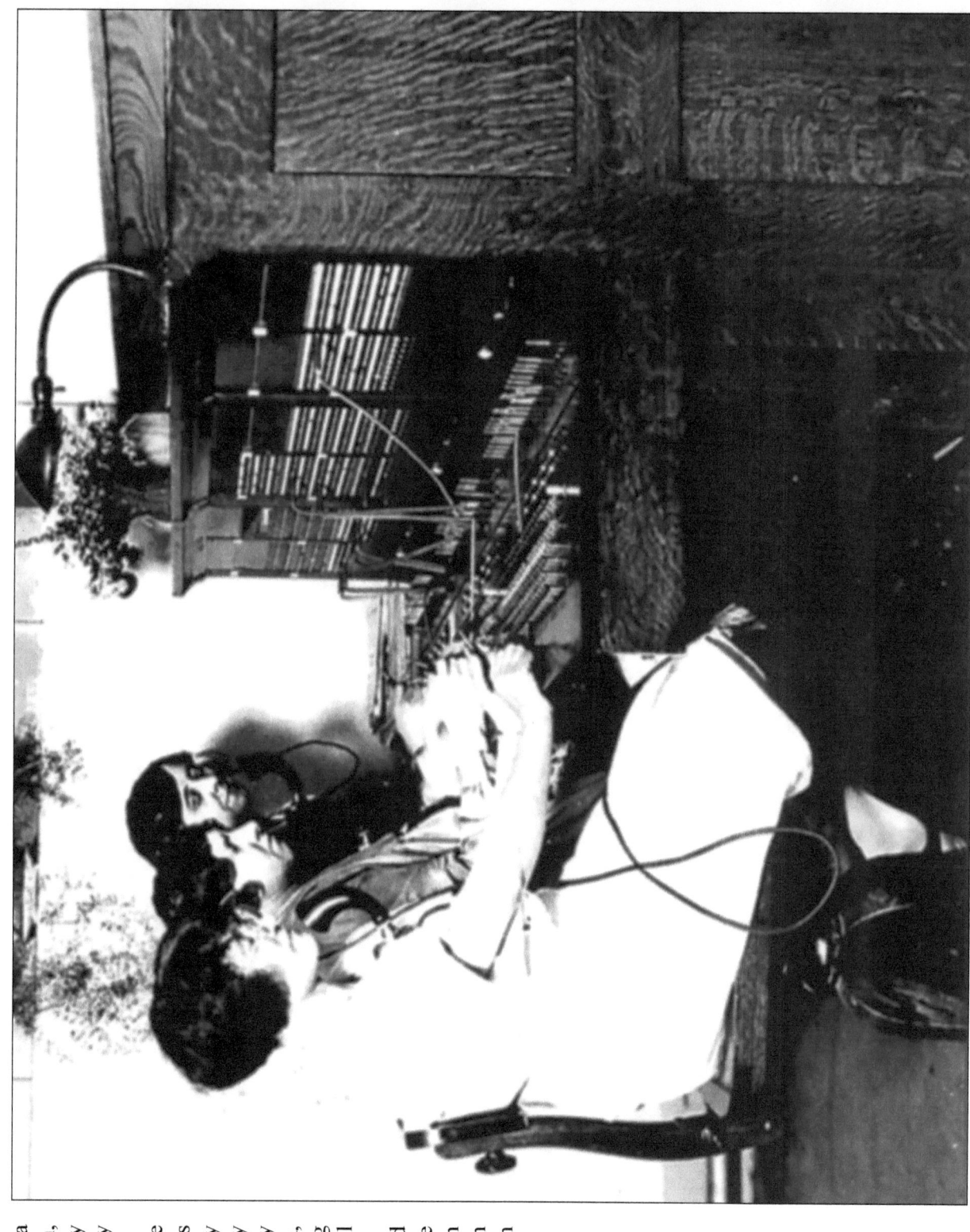

Organized in 1890 with but a single phone in the entire town, the company was formally granted a contract with the City of Hamilton in 1897.

Frank Munsell was a long time manager and his son, C. H. was the company president for many years. In 1928, the company sold to the Middle States Utility Company of Cedar Rapids, Iowa, which had already begun buying up telephone exchanges in small towns in Northern Missouri.

At this time, land was purchased from the Thornton family at the present 2024 site of Levi Garrison and Sons Brewery. The Hamilton exchange would operate through the late 1940s.

HAMILTON FIRE DISTRICT

1957 Hamilton Rural Fire Department. The Hamilton Rural Fire Department was organized in 1951. Leonard Orr served as first president until called to Marine pilot duty. He was followed by Dwight Dodge. Shown standing, left to right were: Lynn Hamlet, J. T. Pawsey, Dwight Dodge, Everett Gurley, Artie Pugh, Charles Stotler and C. A. Ralston. In the truck: Fire Chief E. C. Kavanaugh, Floyd Dunn, Jr.; L. V. Cline, Johnny Wright, Tommy Cline, Larry Allen and Francis Kavanaugh. Not pictured were: Raymond Hartley, Lloyd Bennett and Abe Newkirk. Paul Knudsen served as legal advisor.

Hamilton Fire District. The Hamilton Fire District erected a new all-purpose firehouse in 2012 on South Davis Street.

BREWERY OPENS IN OLD TELEPHONE OFFICE BUILDING

Levi Garrison & Sons. Scott Falke established Levi Garrison & Sons brew pub in 2014 in the historic 1928 Hamilton Telephone Company building. Scott, an Army Reservist with a Ph.D in biochemistry, along with his staff, continues to grow the business. It caters to locals and visitors, as well as a growing distributorship across Northwest Missouri with uniquely named microbrews.

132

JCPenney Boyhood Home

The J. C. Penney Boyhood home was moved to town from the farm east of Hamilton in 1988. It now serves as a museum.

133

A 1940s Buzzer pep club concession stand off of the gymnasium in the old high school/later elementary building. It is site to the Missouri Star Quilt Museum.

134

A. G. Davis Home

The home built in 1875 by town founder Albert Gallatin Davis still stands and is the current residence of the Argyle family on 300 North Prairie. It was known as the "Davis Evergreen Place" because of the evergreens in the yard, one of which survives to this day. The trees were the first planted in Hamilton and they transplanted them to the site of the home when it was built.

A 1912 newspaper says this about the home. "From its earliest incipiency it has been the retreat of old and young where generous hospitality has been dispensed and where good fellowship has reigned. It has been a place where one was free from restraint, least repressed and most spontaneous and natural; a home where welcome awaited its comers; a home where love and duty were guiding stars; a home where precious and sacred memories will live as long as there are those who survive it."

The McBrayer Livery Family

Livery stables, dealing with horses and mules, were essential to early life in Hamilton, and for that matter any small town. Sam McBrayer, and his son, William J. McBrayer, were the biggest dealers in horses and mules in Northwest Missouri from 1875 to around 1920. Sam first operated a livery stable on North Ardinger (called Broadway back then), which would have been just north of today's site of the Community Arts Theater. In later years he operated on East Berry (Mill St.), but his biggest and longest lasting business site was on South Davis where Dollar General in located. The Colby Mercantile Company would eventually buy this property and expand south of their business at the corner of Davis and Berry.

As successful as Sam was, W. J. was even more. It must have been confusing for townsfolk to try to keep track of the number of times the two men bought and sold each other's interests. It was William who built the magnificent sale barn (see page 137) in 1902. The barn measured 110 feet by 300 feet and was high enough to afford loft space for hay and other feed. The lumber was purchased from W. F. Colby at the Colby store. Stephen Scott was foreman for the barn project. It was said that practically ever able bodied man in Hamilton was employed in its construction.

The barn and McBrayer home (the 2023 home of Ron and Jenny Doan of the Missouri Star Quilt Company) were sold to auctioneer F. E. Williams in 1915. Williams would have the barn torn down in 1942.

It was not unusual to have 200 to 300 animals housed in the big barn. McBrayer kept 80 people on his payroll to help look after his interests while he and brothers, Claude (who also operated a coal business on the site of Ed Ernat's machine shop) and Sol, traveled about the Midwest buying animals. Buying transactions sometimes involved cutting checks for as much as $20,000 in a single week's time. At the livery, locals could rent a horse for a day or week, and traveling salesmen with regular routes through Hamilton could do the same.

William was able to latch onto a lucrative government contract delivering horses and mules to the Army during World War I. Even as he stayed busy on the road, McBrayer bought and sold properties in Hamilton, including a large number of the finest homes, a penchant he passed on to Col. Williams.

Eventually, the livery business took a back seat to the advent of the automobile and farm power equipment. Sam died in 1929 and William passed away in 1947.

The McBrayer Barn

137

James M. Kemper Home

Located at 107 North Gallatin, corner of Gallatin and McGaughy streets in west Hamilton, the James Kemper home, though in altered state, is one of the oldest in Hamilton.

James Kemper came to Hamilton from Mirabile in 1859 and clerked in the A. G. Davis store on today's site of the Community Arts Theatre. He moved to Gallatin, where he formed a partnership in a general store with John Ballinger and Samuel P. Cox. His son, William T. Kemper, the Kansas City capitalist, was born in Gallatin in 1867. The Kempers returned to Hamilton in the late 1860s and James operated the Ballinger-Kemper general store before taking charge of his own business on Davis Street.

James built a home in west Hamilton in the period of 1868-69 and his house stood virtually alone in that area at that time. It was a large home, described as a "mansion."

In 1873, James left Hamilton for St. Joseph, where he took a job with the Noyes-Norman Shoe Co. but retained the home in Hamilton. When his wife, the former Sallie Ann Paxton of Mirabile, died in 1875, young son William stayed with Paxton relatives in the Kemper home in Hamilton, and William attended Hamilton school. William rejoined his father when James remarried in 1878.

James sold the Hamilton home in July of 1883 to banker T. D. George, who in turn sold the residence to Judge James Cowgill, a much respected public servant. He was twice elected presiding judge of Caldwell County and was elected to the Missouri legislature in 1890. Cowgill was appointed Railroad and Warehouse Commissioner for Missouri in 1892 and moved to Kansas City in 1893.

In 1900, Cowgill served the first of two terms as Treasurer of Kansas City. In 1908, he was elected Missouri State Treasurer. While

William Kemper

chairman of the State Democratic Central Committee in 1918, Cowgill was elected Mayor of Kansas City. He died in office, at his desk, in 1922.

Cowgill, who was part owner of the Cash-Cowgill brick building at the northwest corner of Davis and Berry streets in Hamilton, sold his residence to Robert Cash in August of 1887. He later sold most of blocks 30 through 33 in the Railroad Addition to Cash in 1902. Cash died in 1905 but his widow, Pattie, continued to live at 107 N. Gallatin until 1916.

With James Kautz, a rural mail carrier, as owner in 1937, a fire in November destroyed the top two floors of the home, which was judged a 75% loss. The home retains its "bones" but today bears little resemblance to the old Kemper mansion, except in the rarely seen arched windows on the ground floor.

The late George Dodge, born in 1905, grew up on the streets of Hamilton and ran errands for many of the businessmen of the day, while

at the same time soaking up the town's history.

According to George, this home did indeed suffer a fire that took off the top two floors of what was a three-story house.

More on James Kemper: In August of 1872, he sold a lot on Ardinger Street to the Presbyterian Society in order for them to build their church. In May of 1874, Kemper sold a lot to the Hamilton Board of Education that allowed more room for the first north side school building. In November of 1875, Kemper sold a lot to M. A. Low on Davis Street that became the site of the Colby Mercantile Company.

James Kemper lived in St. Joseph until 1903, when he moved to Kansas City to be nearer his son, William. He would eventually take up his abode with a daughter in Columbia, Missouri. James died of pneumonia in 1928 at age 87 in San Diego, where he had been living due to ill health.

From Kansas City to Wichita, Ks., and then to Alpine, Tx., the enterprise was beset by problems from the beginning.

Forced into bankruptcy in 1912, the receiver (monetary supporter), William T. Kemper, made a small fortune when oil was discovered under the tracks.

The KCM&O was acquired by the Atchison, Topeka & Santa Fe Railway in 1928, mainly in order to access the West Texas oil fields. The railroad sold the Mexican segments of the railway.

THE MIRABILE CONNECTION

Few small towns can boast of as impressive a business lineage as Hamilton, and it really all began in Mirabile, Missouri. The Partin-Paxton-Penney-Kemper family connection would produce giants in the business world, not just in Hamilton, but nationally and internationally.

James M. Kemper came to Mirabile in March of 1859 but that same year migrated to Hamilton, where he clerked in the store of John Burrows, one of the original town fathers. He slept in the Burrows store on the counters, and while Burrows was postmaster it was his duty to carry mail (at 1 a.m.) from the train station and sort it for the outgoing stagecoach for Lexington.

James went into partnership in the Cox, Ballinger & Kemper store in Gallatin, and that's where his son, William T. Kemper, the Kansas City capitalist, was born in 1867. Returning to Hamilton, James opened a grocery store on today's site of Hy Klas Food & Family Center. The Kempers built a home "on the hill" in west Hamilton. The Kempers left Hamilton for St. Joseph, Mo., in 1873, where he was a traveling salesman for 30 years for a wholesale shoe business.

The wife of James was Sally Paxton, daughter of James Paxton of Mirabile. Sally was a sister of Robert D. Paxton (more on him later). William Partin ran a grocery business in Hamilton in the late 1860s on McGaughy Street. His wife was Elizabeth Penney, sister of James. C. Penney, Sr., and Mrs. A. G. Davis. Partin served as treasurer of the Hamilton School Board in 1874. He raised his family in Hamilton but

Continued on Next Page

KANSAS CITY, MEXICO & ORIENT RAILROAD

Started in 1900 by Arthur Edward Stillwell, the railroad's goal was to reach the Pacific Ocean on the west coast of Mexico at Topolobampoco.

Robert Paxton, another Mirabile boy, had strong financial backing in his business ventures from his nephew, William T. Kemper, who never completed a formal high school education, but would go on to serve as president of the Kansas City Board of Trade and president of the Commerce Trust Company.

In the early 1900s, Robert Paxton leased three stock ranches–in Shreveport, La.; Harper County, Ks.; and southern Oklahoma in the Creek Indian Nation. Near East St. Louis, he was feeding 1,000 head of cattle and 500 head of hogs. Robert and his brother, William, owned a 14,000 acre cattle ranch east of Denver in 1905.

In 1907, Robert and his nephew, Hume, whose life was perhaps worthy of a Brad Pitt movie, went to Mexico, where they would manage a large sugar plantation and a 20,000 acre coffee plantation near Puerto, Mexico. This was during a period of revolt and unrest that would lead to American intervention in 1914. The Mexican Revolution would see the Paxtons flee the country, escaping on the day the Americans took Vera Cruz. They were somehow able to board a German warship and from there transfer to a banana boat, with only the clothes on their backs.

Hume, the nephew of William Partin and Hamilton town founder A. G. Davis, and the cousin of William T. Kemper and retail giant J. C. Penney, returned to Caldwell County and became assistant cashier of the Kingston Exchange Bank, but he soon resigned such a passive existence and served a term of enlistment in the Navy. He contracted typhoid fever while in Mexico in 1915, and in 1918 became deathly ill with the Spanish Flu and pneumonia. He would recover and return to Mexico with his Uncle Robert, but would become ill again in 1923 with sleeping sickness, which was treated in a hospital in El Paso, Tx.

Robert Paxton at one time had a residence on South Ardinger, which he sold in 1900. He lived at times, in Mexico, Louisiana, Topeka, Kansas City and New York Both Paxton men would return often to Hamilton to renew old acquaintances and deliver memorials to the Paxton-Kemper plot at Highland Cemetery.

Mr. and Mrs. Robert D. Paxton

J. C. Penney Sr.

Paxton-Penney-Partin-Kemper

Continued from Previous Page

eventually moved west, where his son, also named William, ended up owning several retail stores.

J. C. Penney, Sr. married his cousin, Mary Francis Paxton, who lived in Kentucky but had traveled to Missouri to visit relatives. When it was time for Mary to return to her home, her escort was J. C. Penney, Sr. On the trip, the two became well acquainted. James remained in Kentucky for a time where he taught school for several terms. The young couple married and remained there until the close of the Civil War, when they bought a farm east of Hamilton where young James Cash Penney was born.

Mary Francis was a cousin of Mrs. A. G. Davis and Elizabeth Partin.

J.C. PENNEY MEMORIAL LIBRARY & MUSEUM

Following the death of retail magnate J. C. Penney, a museum was built in his honor with the help of his nephew, E. R. (Bob) Penney and a local board.

A bust of the late J. C. Penney occupies a prominent spot in the museum, alongside memorabilia of his agriculture and retail accomplishments.

The museum displays were put together with help from the JCPenney Company headquarters in Texas

The J. C. Penney Library has undergone numerous updates, especially in technology, to keep up with changing needs of local clientele.

Mock Wedding. This mid-1950s mock wedding was sponsored by the Hamilton Garden Club. Taking part in the skit were: Janet (Hamlet) Adkison (sitting), Barbara (Hines) McDaniel (background), Larry Hamlet (minister), Ron Hines (groom) and Mary Ellen Miller (bride).

Hamilton Rotary Club – October 10, 1949

STRAND STUDIO

Hamilton Rotary Club. Members of the Hamilton Rotary Club in 1949. Officers that year were: Robert Hampton, president; J. C. Mahoney, vice president; Frances Hunt, secretary; B. A. Hawks, outgoing president and board member; R. E. Neale, board member; and Dr. R. G. Gillilan, board member.

143

CARDINAL LANES BOWLING ALLEY

The grand opening and dedication of Cardinal Lanes was held in October of 1962. The new bowling alley, under the ownership and management of Leo and Marge Leutticke, was erected through the efforts of the Community Improvement Corporation of Hamilton. Over 500 people attended the dedication. Among guest speakers were Mayor L. G. Ehlers and J. C. Penney. A drawing was held and first prize of a new Brunswick bowling ball went to Ralph Blades. Second prize, a pair of bowling shoes, went to Gordon Dale Swindler. Later, John and Louana Catron acquired ownership of the facility and ran it for many years.

144

Hamilton Bowl. Tony and Jessica Miller purchased Cardinal Lanes bowling alley in March of 2022 from AMP and Family LLC. The couple has upgraded the lanes, the masking units, parking lot, kitchen, bathrooms, furnace and many other items. Future expansion is also in their plans.

145

Summer Recreation Sites in Hamilton

Hamilton Municipal Swimming Pool. The American Legion post gave land adjoining Highway 13 to the city of Hamilton for a public park, and this site was planned for the swimming pool. The R-2 School District provided additional land south of Penney High School to accomodate pool plans. Members of the Literary Study Club went house to house to help promote the passage of a $70,000 bond issue, which passed by only 17 votes. Hamilton's swimming pool opened to the public in the summer of 1964. Penney High School science teacher Tom Mounter was the first pool manager. Lifeguards in 1964 were Dana Palmer, Jim Bretz, Eric Elster, Gary Franklin and Randy Ridings. Basket girls were Vicki Baker, Sandra Kinne, Judy Kuhnert and Linda Miller. Richard Johnson was clean up boy. It too, has undergone many changes and renovations.

Hamilton Lake View Golf Course. Originally a sand greens course, Hamilton's Lake View Golf Course opened to the public in 1958. Prior to Lake View, the community's golf course was on the McNary farm just south of town off Highway 13. It, too, was a 9-hole sand green course. Members of the McNary family were still finding stray golf balls on the former course into the 1970s. In June of 1969, an FHA loan was obtained in order to build a clubhouse for Lake View Golf Course. Lawrence Kelmel was the general contractor, with the following subs: Johnson Brothers, concrete; Gordon D. Swindler, painting; Dorson Michael, plumbing; and Forrest Linville, electrical. Officers who helped make the clubhouse project a success were Charles Rouse, Tom Holman, Henry Franklin, Ross Hicklin, Dean Trosper and George Pugh. The present course has undergone changes over the years, including a transition to grass greens and expansion to the west of the original course.

MEMORIAL DAY IN HAMILTON, 1888

Hamilton residents first observed Memorial Day on May 30, 1888. Civil War veterans met in the office of J. D. Van Valkenburg (south corner of present Sewing Center) to take steps to hold decoration services for the first time in Hamilton. Gideon Prentice was chosen president on that day; Rev. R. J. Mathews, chaplain; Rev. I. S. Ware, orator; Col. J. W. Harper, marshal; Major Harve Farabee, assistant marshal; and an executive committee of J. J. Hooker, George Naugle and William Wagenseler.

A precession formed on Decoration Day in front of the Methodist Church, led by the Hamilton Cornet Band, orator of the day, old soldiers on foot and citizens on foot and in carriages. The procession went to the cemetery where music was provided by the band and a choral club, followed by a prayer from Rev. Mathews and oration by Rev. Ware.

Col. Harper led a group of veterans who decorated the graves of 18 Civil War veterans who were buried both in the old Rohrbough and the new Highland cemeteries. According to a newspaper account of the day, 47 veterans at the service and about 1,000 people from the town and community.

In those days, every soldier's grave had a bouquet of flowers placed on it, made by the women of the old soldiers' families. The American Legion post took charge of ceremonies at Highland Cemetery following its formation.

Origin of Memorial Day

Early in 1866, a Mrs. A. W. Howard, widow of a Confederate officer, suggested the setting apart of a day for placing flowers on graves of Confederate soldiers. The idea was well received and April 26, that year, was made the occasion for the first memorial observances.

This southern idea appealed to the men and women of the north, as well. In 1868, Gen. John A. Logan, then nation commander of the Grand Army of the Republic, issued an order calling for Memorial Day exercises on May 30. This date was retained as the time for the annual decoration of Union soldiers' graves and public commemoration of the lives and deeds of the men in blue. For many years, ex-Confederates continued to observe April 26.

The following poem, by Henry Wadsworth Longfellow, was written in 1882:

Sleep comrades, sleep and rest
On this field of the grounded arms.
Where foes no more molest,
Nor sentry's shot alarms.

Ye have slept on the ground before
And started to your feet
At the sound of cannon's sudden roar.
Or the drum's redoubling beat.

But in this camp of death
No sound your slumber breaks.
Here is no fevered breath,
No wound that bleeds and aches.

All is repose and peace.
Untrampled lies the sod.
The shouts of battle cease.
As sentinels to keep

Your rest from danger free.
Your silent tents of green
We deck with fragrant flowers.
Yours has the suffering been.
The memory shall be ours.

It is the truce of God.
Rest comrades, rest and sleep.
The thoughts of men shall be

From the Chosin Reservoir to Bastogne and Corregidor...
From the Gulf of Tonkin to the Fall of Saigon...

Thomas Watson
Civil War
140th Illinois Inf.

W. J. Ervin
Civil War
3rd Mo. Inf. CSA

Hugh Smylie
Civil War
98th Oh. Inf.

C. C. Green
Civil War
32nd Wisc. Inf.

Sherman Henkins
World War I

John Craven
World War I

Charles McBride
World War I

Benjamin Clark
World War I

148

Clayton Snyder
Korea

John Lee
Korea

Al Smith
Korea

Leonard Orr
Korea & Viet Nam

David Hicklin
Viet Nam

Roger Dixon
Viet Nam

Ron Yoakum
Viet Nam

Editor's Note: There are over 3,000 military veterans buried in Highland Cemetery, so it would be impossible to include all in this Memorial Day tribute. However, these pages are dedicated to all, named and unnamed, who served this country in times of need, and came back to Hamilton to their final resting places.

149

THE GREATEST GENERATION

Frank & Helen Daley
World War II - Europe

Lyle Daley
World War I & II

Dean Ayers
World War II - Europe

Leslie Sweany
World War II - Pacific

Dorothea Engel
World War II - Pacific

Dale Oldfield
World War II - Pacific

Robert Hines
World War II - Pacific

Elmo Smith
World War II - Europe

William Kuhnert
World War II - Europe

E. T. Strade
World War II - North Africa

Elmo Smith
World War II - Europe

Hales Family. The extended family of the late Dean and Dixie (Connor) Hales gathered on March 31, 2024 at the J. C. Penney Boyhood home with the 1947 Cadillac, at one time owned by J. C. Penney. Photo taken in remembrance of the late Kandi (Hales) Railsback.

151

HAMILTON SESQUICENTENNIAL

The Hamilton community came together en masse in 2005 for a unique photo on the occasion of the 150th anniversary of the town's founding. The photo was taken from the roof of The Hamilton Bank by photographer Tom Strade.